MW00477938

FOR THE LOVE OF MOUNTAIN BIKING

James McArthur

FOR THE LOVE OF MOUNTAIN BIKING

Published by: J.McArthur

www.jamesie.life

ISBN

PB ISBN 978-2-9593885-0-7
HB ISBN 978-2-9593885-1-4
EBOOK ISBN 978-2-9593885-2-1

I lifted the front of my new mini-skirt (the skirt formerly known as shorts) and gave him a flash of the carnage beneath. He immediately stopped chewing, looked down, and started packing away his lunch.

"OK... Zat is definitely an emergency," he said. "Let's go now."

"Hey... No... It's alright Dr," I said, "I can wait a few minutes, no problem. Please, finish your lunch first..."

"It's OK," he said, looking up at me with a face two shades pastier than 10 seconds earlier, "I am no longer 'ungry..."

"Oops. Sorry Doc."

-

For the Love of Mountain Biking is a smorgasbord of engaging stories, perceptive observations and amusing anecdotes in tribute to the sport we love. They blend into a lively narrative, inspired by the author's own experiences and BIG love for mountain biking.

It's an appreciation of the places we go, the people we meet, the journey it takes us on and all the great times along the way. It stirs emotions, stokes nostalgia and reignites those peak sensations. It makes you want to get right up, go for a ride and send it!

From growing up by the Howgill Fells in the Yorkshire Dales to living and riding in the vast Portes du Soleil bike park network, James shares his perspective in a true celebration of mountain biking. He offers useful insights, exploring the essence of the sport and why we love to ride… And if you don't ride already, you might just fall in love with it anyway.

To my family.

Love you guys. x

Contents

1 - Introduction

Going for a ride crosses your mind. Maybe somebody mentioned one, maybe you watched a vid, maybe it just popped in there, or maybe you've got a little window of opportunity coming up, where you could just squeeze one in…

And so it begins…

A pervasive, gnawing, niggle in the back of your mind. It's a whisper at first, *"Doo it, doo it, doo it."*

Your bike wants it too. It knows. Its ears pricked up and its headset tilted like a dog and someone shouted, "Walkies!" But it's telepathic… You didn't even have to say a word and it knew. It knows what you're thinking and it wants it. It wants it just as much as you do. You're connected… And when you're riding, you are *one!*

"Doo it, doo it, doo it." The little voice is getting louder, it's growing assertive. Its message is starting to percolate through the soft spongy grey matter inside your head.

Its tentacles of influence are snaking through your neural pathways, occupying more and more of your mental computing power. It's stifling normal cognitive service like a zombie grub at the control panel of a caterpillar.

"Doo it, doo it, doo it."

It's a double whammy though, triple whammy even. Your heart was in it before your mind even got involved. Your heart is automatically drawn to the things that bring it love, joy and good feelings. It's just sitting there, pumping away, patiently doing its thing, waiting for an executive decision from above and a green light to *go, go, go!*

The rest of your body's ready for a hit as well. A hit of dopamine, serotonin and all those other feel-good chemicals. The Walter White neurons are on standby. They're ready to start cooking up a chemical cocktail and distributing it, to give every fibre of your being a buzz from the good stuff.

"Doo it, doo it" takes a step back from the spotlight for a moment and lets reasoning step forward for its five minutes in the frame, *"Hey... I get it. I know 'Doo it, doo it' can be a bit much, especially when you've other things to be getting on with, buuut it's not going to go away any time soon and you're not being productive anyway... There's no point in staying here, making limited progress, only to wish that you'd gone later on... Don't forget, it's great exercise, it's good for your head and your well-being... You'll probably be even more productive once you've been for a ride and got it out of your system... Just sayin'."*

"Doo it, doo it, doo it!"

"Sod it! I'm in! Let's go! WAHOO!"

There are loads of us around the world that know this feeling and this is pretty much where this book started. I live in The Portes du Soleil in France and as soon as the bike parks and lifts open for summer, I find it nigh-on impossible to concentrate on anything else if I don't get a regular fix.

As this year's bike season started to ramp up and I struggled to concentrate on other things, I thought, "You know what?.. If I write a book about mountain biking, that'll potentially make going riding and anything else bike-related 'work-related'. And, if it goes well, I might be able to do more books and more biking!"

Let's see how that goes.

I started collecting and polishing stories, anecdotes and other stuff from my time riding. From growing up near the excellent riding in the Howgill Fells and the Lake District to my current home in the French Alps. I explored my own perspectives to try and capture the essence of the sport we love. I hoped to create something that would strike a chord with you, my fellow riders.

I hope you enjoy it.

2 - Linking It Up

"Right Jimbo! It's time to link this bad boy up…"

Another torrent of sweat dribbles down my back and disappears into the back of my pants. The chances of any of that moisture actually evaporating and providing a cooling effect, are totally scuppered by my back protector. It's there to protect my back from a certain amount of potential damage but also, as it turns out, from fresh air and cooling!

It's so hot that I can physically feel the waves of dry heat pulsing through the air. It's a scorcher for sure. The sun's rays begin to prickle the back of my un-creamed neck and remind me that for its sake, the sooner I'm back in the shade of the woods, the better. The emerald green water in the reservoir just a stone's throw to my right looks pretty tempting but I've got business to attend to.

I run a gloved finger over the face of my goggles to clear the fresh coating of dust scooped out of the air on the last run. Peace is interrupted as the *clatter* of chains and *whoomph* of tyres rise into earshot behind me. A small group of riders race out of the trees and up onto the track that skirts the top of the reservoir banks. They pause for a chat.

It's Les Gets, Dans L'Gaz, Summer 2023. The shapers have made changes to this old favourite black trail that snakes down the south face of Mont Chéry It criss-crosses the World Cup track as it goes. I know what's in store now and I'm ready to try and tick off a clean top-to-bottom run.

"OK! Time to get into this before these guys get to me and while it's still clear ahead."

A quick glance down to the front axle confirms the through bolt is sitting tight. I open my right knee and peep back through to check the rear one's looking solid too. Properly connected wheels are always high on my "pre-flight" checks priority list.

A glance back over my shoulder confirms the new arrivals have stopped for a quick breather. I heave my weight up off the seat, first onto one pedal, then the other, level them up and balance for a second. I shift my weight forward with three big pedal cranks, tilting the bike from side to side for maximum downward force and forward momentum.

The burst of acceleration rolls me quickly towards the lip of the reservoir bank. The first sandy-coloured double jump comes into view. A ribbon of worn dirt leads the way to it. I suck the bike up towards me as I dip over the outside lip of the reservoir and pump down the face of the bank, past the trail sign and prepare for take off!

This jump always looks a little "pingy"... (*Actually, I should probably mention that there are words/phrases in here that are specific to mountain biking, local vernacular or that I've shamelessly made up. If the context doesn't give you a clue to the meaning, I've slapped a glossary at the back of the book to lend a hand.*)

Anyway... This jump always looks pingy and *scoof*. I'm airborne and a little early tension in my body sends me further left than I wanted but the smooth silence of momentary flight and the turbulent, cooling air gushing into the face of my helmet feel great already.

A quick kink right on landing corrects the poor flight trajectory and plops me into the rut that thousands of mountain bike tyres have gradually eroded. It's a straight shot past the left of the tree, over a surface of roots and exposed bedrock. Let it roll, then a quick dab of the brakes before stepping down off the last sloping slab and hook the wheels into the left-hander.

Fast, rough, grey, rocky, rollercoaster berms get the bike's suspension and my arms working hard. Left, right, left, right, left, right, left. My vision darts ahead, tracing the line, picking out hazards to make split-second adjustments. Guiding the tyres between the most vicious-looking rocks to keep them rolling smoothly, moving fast and fully inflated.

The berms uncoil, straightening up and accelerating my mass. The trail tracks left, unweighting over a little roller and on, to a new floaty double jump that begs for a whip.

"*Wahoo!*"

Keep the landing nice and tight to set up for a small fade to the right, over the roots and slot nicely into the channel between raised tree stumps. Off the brakes and *bap, bap, bap* over the thick round dusty root limbs, A little pop and point it at the entrance of the fast dusty berm ahead.

SHRALP go the tyres as I dive into the corner. Not intentionally. I just got into that one way too hot and on the limit of grip. "*Yes though! Come on!*" Tiptoeing on the limit of speed and control is maximum engagement and maximum buzz. Those limits might well be at different points for all of us but we're all getting the exact same sensational sensations when we're blipping our own personal limiters.

Two smooth, compacted berms follow in each direction. I take a little cautionary glance up and to the left as I enter the last right-hander. A version of the World Cup track has run alongside here in the past, before gapping across it. People freeride it from time to time and there's the potential for a collision.

After the glance, I've got a couple of step-down/double jumps to tackle before the left-hander. This is where the aerial intersection and potential collision, might take place. I learned that the early glance was worthwhile after an *extremely* near miss one time, when someone's wheels sailed past, just behind my head!

All clear(!) this time and I dive into the left-hander, then a quick right and engage launch mode. We're back on another World Cup variant and off the brakes for a big straight gap.

The trail arcs right before another unnerving-looking gap followed by a right-hander shark-fin style take off. It looks like someone just grabbed a digital version of the berm exit, clicked on the end and dragged it into the air.

No sooner have I landed, but I'm up again and skimming over a tabletop, peppered with embedded rocks. I watch the last one fly beneath and set the wheels back down on terra firma and straight into a big compression. *"Oof!"*

The compression and rebound are crammed into a split second and I'm pinged back out of the dip and off the next take off with very little say in the matter.

My eyes widen for a split second as I assess and hope that the ping hasn't fired me way off line but it's all good. *"At ease eyes."* I'm soaring straight for a sweet, high entrance on the berm ahead and touchdown! Eyes left, tracking ahead around the corner and *Scccrrruuuch!*

"Let 'er rip Jimbo and open it up for the straight." There's a hip to the left, landing high in the bank, a double after that, then a right-left chicane. I've only gone and hooked up a lovely hole shot off the new berm which has fired me perfectly, fast, up and to the left.

"Hold your nerve, Jim lad." Hug left, balance the weight, keep the grip and dance across the rise and left of the trees. Straight line through, stay tight and *Brap-brap-bap-bap-bap* over the roots.

Skiff! Brushed the tree with my elbow. *"Phew! That was close."* The roots and the ground drop away in front of me. Look left. There's a new, thin, high line that the World Cup riders have cut in. It's above the main line on the right. *"Guide that front wheel and I'm in!"* Granted, I'm carrying a fraction of the speed of the World Cup big dogs but I'm in, and on a good line for a fast entry to the next straight.

Off the brakes again and a few big pedal cranks just be on the safe side and *"Send it!"* It's a lovely, long, floaty send on this jump. It looks sketchy on the approach but it's much easier to clear than it looks and it feels great to make the landing, nice and clean. There's even time for a quick pause for breath in the air, a bit of a grin and touchdown!

A left-banking shark's fin reels in fast from up ahead. The latest version of the World Cup track hips the right-hand side of the landing here and drops off back into the woods but I'm carrying speed and cutting left, saving the momentum for another pingy double, *"Wahoo!"* Then I'm out of the woods, onto the ski piste and back in the sunshine.

No time to enjoy the weather though, it's time to intensify the workout. Straight into the first set of tight berms on the open ski piste. High and early into the first one, wheels railing just beneath the grassy turf lip at the top then *Vrap!* round to the right, unweighting the bike after the compression of the corner and shifting it to follow the shortest path to the bank of the next left-hander.

Vrap!… Vrap, vrap, vrap! Left, right, left, right, left, right, left. My head's level and following the straightest line possible down the middle of the snaking track. Eyes front, picking out each entrance, apex, and exit. My vision always tracking a couple of steps ahead of the action.

The bike pendulums beneath my head and shoulders following the contours of the track. I've lost count of the times I've ridden this section but it always feels like they've added a couple more berms since the last time I rode it.

Then *whoompf!* Off the brakes through the final berm and accelerate out across the clearing. Gravity grabs me by the scruff of the neck and slings me downwards.

My tyres break contact with the ground momentarily over the humped contour of rough earth, bringing a flashing glimpse of peace and quiet. Then it's shattered as tyres and earth are reunited a moment later and not a second too soon so that I can grab a big handful of brakes before the next right-hand corner.

The tyres scrabble, chatter and chew for grip to wash off speed. My body opens to the right and my hips move out to the left, weighting the outside of the bike and lowering the centre of gravity as I skitter around a flatter right-hand corner. I'm battling hard to try and hold speed for the left-right and the new gap that follows.

My mind jumps nostalgically for a second to the trees and roots that used to frame this section. I preferred it when they were here. *"Never mind that now divvy! Get your head back in the game!"*

The next gap rears up and a high-speed mental calculation gives me the green light to commit. The take-off is cambered one way with the landing the other… *"Have I got enough speed? Just stay off those brakes and a big pull to make sure. Phew! Yeah buddy!"*

I bank left and into a section lined with the remnants of more of those trees. A super-sized stubble patch of freshly cut tree stumps line the steepest kicker of the whole trail.

This jump schiz-ed me out for the first few attempts. The steep take-off and missing trees make it feel like you're very exposed and launching vertically into oblivion.

It feels so steep that there's a stalling sensation at the peak of the jump-arc. Like a cartoon character sprinting motionless in the air, before gravity is re-engaged and downward acceleration resumes.

Time for bigger, steeper, deeper berm-age all the way to the bottom. The shaping crew has even cut in a couple of new gap jumps in this section to raise the stakes.

I fade left, to get a high entry into the next, steep, right-hand berm and to allow gravity to rub off some of my speed. I turn in, dropping fast and round to the right. *Sccccrrruunch!*

"Stay high, Jamesie boy! Don't be tempted to drop into the corner too soon and arrive in the dust pile three quarters of the way round. Get into that berm nice and early, high to the right and rail it, smooth and fast baby! Yes!"

Sccccrrrrunch!, Sccccrrrrucnh! left, right.

The right-hander shrinks behind me and I roll up the face of a small table top. The momentary deceleration gives me a split second to glance left and see my nemesis. This is one of the new gaps in this section. I'm not a fan. It's very close to the exit of the berm. There's a cambered take off, requiring you to pivot in the air and land the other way.

It always feels like there's a lot to deal with in a short amount of time and space. All of it with the added pressure to carry the necessary speed and… *"Flaps! I've psyched myself out."* I'm already in the berm and my fingers have staged a coup and braked! I've bottled it!

"Awww! Freakin' bum-sticks... Dammit!"

"So close!"

I pick up speed again through the next few berms and mentally beat myself up with disappointment.

The track has been baked hard down here in the open. Out of the shade of the trees and in the full glare of the summer sun, the ground is parched. Hundreds of tyres have picked and scraped away at the crusty coating, before blowing through and liberating vast reserves of soft dust below. The dirt has been pummelled and pounded, ground smaller and smaller. It's so fine, some of it is still hanging in the air from the last person down. I gather another scoop-full on the surface of my goggles, in my nostrils, and crack on.

I reach the next of the new gaps a few berms later but I've already made the conscious decision to skip it. The flow's been interrupted. My head's not in the right place now and I just need to let it go and regroup. I roll the gap awkwardly, almost making violent contact between my chest and the bars, before trundling into the final few berms.

I suck up another compression at the bottom, which always seems to catch me out. I wince internally and simultaneously pray that nobody's about to wipe me out from the right.

Whilst it's a slim one, there's always a chance that someone is riding the line of the (closed) World Cup track which intersects Dans L'Gaz again. I'm always a bit nervous that someone might just be blatting across the meadow traverse at full chat.

It's all clear though, and all good, so I squash out the roller following the intersection and grab a handful of brakes before turning left onto the little wooden bridge. The squelch of the honeycomb, anti-slip, rubber matting makes for a pleasant change of sensation. I pre-hop the end of the bridge just for the fun of it and land on the transition.

That's it. Job done... Well... Not quite done but almost done and I'm done... For today anyway.

There is a little bit more track at the bottom that links back to Mont Chéry lift station from here. It's under construction at the moment but even when it's not, it's designed to be ridden as part of the World Cup track and doesn't ride well with the lower speed entering from this road crossing.

I opt for a roll down the road this time and make a beeline for an ice cream to cool down. A clean top to bottom of Dans L'Gaz will have to wait for another day.

3 - BIG Love

I'm a fan, obviously, but even when you take bias out of the equation and look at things impartially, I reckon there's a pretty solid argument that mountain biking might just be, the best sport *ever*!

There are so many aspects to mountain biking, so many benefits and so many outstanding contradictions that I can't help thinking, it might just have it all.

You're already reading this, so it's highly likely that you feel the same way, but it's always nice to have a bit of a love-in. I'll be peppering this book with many excellent points to contribute to the cast-iron case for mountain biking's supremacy. Allow me to expand on that for a few moments though and please join me on fist-bumping, hell-yeah-ing love-in of Fox 40 proportions!

For most of us, this love affair has blazed within for a long-long time. It was probably sparked into existence when we wobbled, weaved and nervously cranked those first few pedal strokes in life... And then you're off!

And you *are* off... FREEDOM!.. Freedom, friends, good times and play... Emotionally-charged cerebral, physical and sensory memories are branded onto the subconscious mind, for life!.. *Sizzle!*

I still feel like that same kid when I'm playing out on bikes. Whether I'm on my own or with my mates and now with *my* kids, and *their* mates. Class! I fully intend to impress

14

any grandkids with a trick or two in the future but let's not get *way* ahead of myself.

If I'm not very much mistaken, that vibe percolates right to the top of the sport. Beneath the pressure, the dedication, the competition and the razzmatazz, it *does* seem like most of those top riders are still big kids, playing out on bikes, with their mates... And getting paid for it.

> *"Mum! I want to be a mountain biker when I grow up."*
> *"Well, you'll have to choose honey, because you can't do both."*

Those first few pedal turns set the wheels in motion for a life-long pursuit of personal progression. First come wheelies, bunny-hops, "look mum, no hands". Next, you're lining your mates up on the floor to see how many you can jump over from a scaffold plank ramp.

Then come the trails and the woods and the mountains. Those feelings as your confidence grows. You're looking further ahead, riding faster and steeper. Refining your technique and improving your body position. You're sending the jumps rather than braking and squashing, relaxing into the flow as the dots connect, pumping for speed, accelerating through corners and daring to commit.

Adding the personal style, the tweaks, the tricks, the whips and the flow. Ticking off the features and challenges as you go. Experimenting with lines. Blasting over obstacles that once were a dream. Getting faster, bigger, smoother and cleaner.

It's playing out wherever or however you're riding. It's playing out if you're with your mates and it's playing out when you're on your own. I'm no spring chicken but I can still happily spend hours in a car park practising wheelies, manuals, endos, riding backwards, balancing, whatever, without a care in the world.

In fact, just a couple of weeks ago, I tried a one-handed wheelie for the first time ever and guess what?.. I did it!.. *"Come on!.. Get in!.. Still improving!.."* My 12 year old was well impressed. That right there, that is the absolute sugar!

When you peel back the layers of time, responsibility and life experience, it's just that exact same soul, enjoying that exact same simple joy.

4 - Planting the Seed

I grew up in a small village called Sedbergh in the North of England. Despite being in the county of Cumbria, Sedbergh lies just within the western boundaries of the Yorkshire Dales National Park. It's also just a few miles from the eastern edge of the Lake District National Park.

The village nestles in the valley at the foot of the beautiful Howgill Fells. It sits on a geographical palm, with valley fingers stretching out towards Tebay, Kirkby Stephen, Hawes, Dent and Kirkby Lonsdale. These dales dissect and divide even more hilltop high-ground as they go.

If you've ever driven up the stretch of M6 motorway between Kendal and Tebay, the Earth's crust rears up on either side of the tarmac. The motorway is squeezed into a meandering route between the huge haunches to its left and right.

As you gaze up at the rolling summits of the Howgill Fells to the east, their shoulders, flanks and folds look like a herd of giant slumbering elephants who've been napping there for millennia. Admittedly, I've not driven every mile of it but I reckon this could be the most beautiful stretch of motorway in the whole of the UK.

Needless to say, with all the mountains, fells and wild countryside in the area, there's an abundance of great mountain biking on offer.

We moved to Sedbergh when I was about four years old. My folks had been moving around, following job opportunities in their teaching careers and one of those opportunities had led them to Sedbergh.

They've always both loved the outdoors, mountains and the natural world so Sedbergh ticked a whole bunch of wish-list boxes as a great place to live. It was fantastic for all kinds of outdoor sports. Believe it or not, there was even enough snow in the winter back then for a cross-country ski-rental business to exist, just up the road at Cautley.

I had no idea at the time but that move and my dad's new job would deliver a whole bunch of bike-related benefits for me, ones that I'd have the good fortune to enjoy in the upcoming years.

He had started his career as a PE teacher and after working hard, gaining qualifications, making moves and taking promotions, he'd landed this new job as a headteacher.

He'd been drawn to schools which specialised in educating kids with educational and behavioural problems. He'd always felt a natural affinity with these kids who had been excluded from mainstream schools and who faced a whole different set of challenges.

There was the odd, legit "little turd" there but most of them were really good lads. Many of them had just been dealt a crappy hand in life or had reasons why they struggled to conform to the "norm".

In a village with a population of less than 3,000, Sedbergh was home to no less than four schools at the time. There was the local primary school where my mum ended up teaching, a small secondary comprehensive school (without a sixth form) and there was the large and prestigious independent, Sedbergh School, renowned for its rugby-playing prowess. Then, there was my dad's school.

Like the private school, his was residential. The boys would stay in dorms throughout term time and go home for the odd weekend and during the holidays. Numerous staff lived on site and seeing as dad was the big boss, we lived in a house on the grounds as well.

That school got a lot of my dad's time and attention but there was a beneficial trade-off… My mates and I got an awesome space to play out. At the time and in our eyes, it was essentially a bike park, before bike parks even existed!

On plan, the school grounds were shaped like an "L". They were situated on a sloping site that rose up from the main road out of Sedbergh. The road ran along the southern boundary at the base of the L.

Next to the road at the bottom was a football pitch, which had been cut and filled level. Above that, a bank sloped all the way up to the main residential building, sitting on another level plateau maybe 50 metres above.

The main residential building was a grand-looking, Victorian structure with steep pitched red-tiled roofs. It had originally opened as a girls' school at the turn of the 19th century. It had then been used as a military training facility during World War II, before being converted into a special school for boys in the 1970s.

The bank leading up to it had an open grassed area to the left with a few trees and a big, beautiful rhododendron bush. This whole area would erupt into a spray of yellow when the daffodils burst into life in the spring. They were closely tailed by a blanket of blue in the steeper woodland section to the right when the bluebells followed suit.

Behind and above the residential building at the top of the site were another grassed area, parking, garages and three houses. One of these was ours.

A tarmac driveway climbed the length of the western boundary of the site with another strip of woodland padding to its left. The road branched off twice to the right – once to a parking area in front of the residential building and once again behind it, where it formed a turning loop in front of our houses.

Back down at main-road level, at the end of the football pitch and at the toe of the "L", lay another collection of buildings. The education block was down there, as well as three more staff houses, a gym, a tennis court and another access point from the main road.

A stepped path ran up from the education block, through the steeper woodland section and to the residential block. It accessed the front and also continued alongside the eastern boundary and around the back to our house.

One of my mates lived close by on a farm. He was a couple of years older than me and he, and my dad, had actually taught me how to ride a bike right there in front of our house. I remember my mate encouraging me to set off again and again down a slope behind the residential building, first with just one stabiliser, then with none.

I remember the excitement of getting the hang of it and the exhilaration of getting faster and faster. Then, I remember my first introduction to target fixation, as I headed straight for a dismantled concrete coal bunker, before going straight over the bars and head first into it.

Helmets weren't really a thing in those days.

I also remember going to the doctor *and* I remember the stitches being sewn into my eyebrow. I do remember being told I'd also got a concussion but I don't remember asking my mum what was for tea and what time the A-Team was going to be on, 5000 times that evening.

I was off though! We were off! More friends from primary school ditched the stabilisers and the progression began. Breeze block jumps, see-saws, wheelies, no hands, bunny hops, game on!

We had loads of options for descents too. We could pick up speed on the hard standing near our house, drop onto the lawn next to my dad's office, roll down the bank, gap the flower bed, cross the drive, bunny hop the drainage gulley, skid down the bank, pop off the kicker that had formed where tree roots had raised the ground, then send it off the cutting onto the football pitch. Just thinking about that big drop-to-flat now, with no suspension, makes my knees wince.

I can picture the details of those lines as if I rode them yesterday… I can see it now…

"Muuum!.. I'm off to Ken's!"

"OK!.. Come back at 7!"

I roll my wrist over and set the alarm on my Casio digital watch to 7.00 pm. I close the frosted, two-pane, glass-panelled front door behind me and slip on my green Dunlop wellies (The Five Tens of the Day).

No helmet, no need, no idea back then, even after the coal bunker!

I walk down the curved concrete flagged path to the big brown garden gate and get a whiff of creosote. The real aroma had long since subsided but it had smelt so good when I helped my dad paint it that I get a smell flashback every time I look at it. I double back on myself to the right and into the open garage to grab my trusty steed.

It was a bike. No idea what make it was and I don't even know how you'd classify it nowadays but back then, it was a quiver killer. It'd do whatever it was asked to do.

I swing a leg over, make a left, straighten up and crunch over a narrow gravel bed. A few pedal strokes take me across the hard-standing behind the residential buildings. The right crank arm makes a familiar shing-shing-shing, every time it passes by the shiny metal chain guard, like a chef sharpening his steel. I can bend it out of the way but it bends back in no time so it's not worth the effort.

It's time to dip right, into the real action, tracing the route down the eastern boundary to the educational buildings. I roll down the first few flagstones of the sloped, paved path to build some speed then take a little chink to the left to dip down the steep grass bank for a smooth burst of acceleration and to avoid the steps.

I hop back onto the path and pedal, pedal, pedal along the flat straight. The path makes a right-angle turn to the left up ahead but I cut diagonally across the grass and set up for the best bit.

I point the front wheel to the left of the top step of a steep bank of 5. I tuck it into a narrow rut to the left of the steps and to the right of a small rocky outcrop. Whoomph! I jink back onto a small landing on the path and immediately off the other side to slot into another eroded rut alongside the second bank of steps Whoomph! I pop back onto the path off the brakes and jump the next two long steps then pump right again back onto the grass banking.

At the bottom, ahead of me, is what looks like an ancient boundary of some kind. A row of trees runs horizontally across the whole site at this level, and in between each tree is a raised bank. It looks like the remains of a wall that has been buried by years of debris and rotting veg matter. Grass has eventually taken root, knitted it together and smoothed the whole thing out.

It doesn't matter what it had been, what it is now is a terrific jump and this particular opening between the trees raises even more towards the tree at its right-hand end where the roots have added an extra hit of spice to the lip. Extra height! "Wahoo! Yeah, buddy!"

Actually. I wouldn't have said "Yeah buddy!" in those days. It would more likely have been "Ace!", "Mega!" or our own original "Manifesta!" which we made up completely.

Not much time to regroup before the small bank of "fill", back up onto the football pitch and a chance for a bit more air. "Yes!" Cut the pitch corner, down behind the goal, over the cinder-track long-jump run-up and stitch through the big pine trees alongside the tennis court, through the gate, onto the road and off to Ken's. "Ace!"

We had loads of lines and loads of fun on those grounds. They weren't massive but then neither were we. As we outgrew our starter bikes, pretty much everyone our age ended up with a brilliant new Raleigh Striker for Christmas of the same year. Then, a year or two later, Father Christmas upgraded us all to a Raleigh Burner BMX. Now you're talking!

As we got older, we'd ride further afield. Some of Ken's fell-side fields had nice little rolling jump lines that we'd spot while moving his sheep or cows around. We'd go back with our bikes and push up to try them out.

Great times!

Then, mountain bikes became an actual thing! We'd already been mountain biking on anything with two wheels that would roll down a hill but now there was a specific tool for the job with a name to match!.. We needed them!

Suspension still wasn't even a concept but wide bars, bigger wheels, bigger tyres, and gears, all looked like they'd deliver more speed, more amplitude, more options, and more fun!

I put the Christmas order in… It didn't come. I hadn't outgrown the last bike yet. *"Dammit!"* My little brother got one though, which stung a bit.

I tried to be patient and eventually my time came, and my dad got himself one as well. Let's go!

And what had I received, you might be wondering?..

Wait for it…

A Peugeot!..

A what now?..

Yep… A Peugeot.

And it was freakin' awesome! It was so much fun to ride and so capable. It did what I was hoping it would do and it was everything I was hoping it would be.

I just Googled "Peugeot mountain bikes" to see if I could find an image of that bike and it turns out that Peugeot still makes mountain bikes! Who knew?.. It doesn't look like they've moved on that much though, to be fair.

We started venturing further into the hills. I spent many a traumatising day, trying to hold back tears, as I struggled to push that big lump up a hill 20m behind my dad. No wonder I prefer riding downhill! Haha!

But the descents… I loved them. Tearing down from the top of Arant Haw or The Calf on the roof of the Howgills. Hurtling down from the peak of Winder which dominates the skyline above the Sedbergh. Swinging down onto the footpath running alongside Settlebeck Gill, cutting between the haunches of Winder and its smaller neighbour, Crook.

That run was fast and flowy from the top, then peaty, stepped, rutty and technical. Some nice single-track linked things up before the swing gate at the fell wall. Below that, a stoney, gravely path peppered with little roots, banks and rocks kept the pops coming and the grins going all the way right to my back door! Jammy git!

Then there was the full charge, wide-open descent, down the grassy path on the western flank, from the summit of Winder. It was fast and fun with a big sweeping off-camber right-hander near the bottom. If there'd been a drizzle of rain on that grassy corner it was slicker than a wet-lubed Slip'n'Slide. I only had to high-speed, low-side into the bracken once to get the message that a little more respect and finesse were required.

Another big favourite was a traverse from Sedbergh round to Cautley Spout, the highest single-pitch waterfall in the UK no less! The traverse roughly follows the "fell wall" which is the barrier between fields and farmland below and open fells above.

The last section of this ride was a lengthy, full-chat descent – shaley and rutted single-track darting among the gorse bushes. It was dotted with a minefield of soft, boggy patches that threatened to grab hold of your front wheel and fling you over the bars if you weren't fully switched on. It never failed to put the biggest grin on my face.

We'd take the bikes all over the place: Grisedale, The Dales, The Lake District, holidays in Scotland. We loved it!

Life went on though. I went to secondary school and I upgraded to a Scott WindRiver. I still rode now and again but more things were happening. More things that weren't mountain biking. More school sports and more school work. Different schools, new friends and new interests: skateboarding, rugby, music, drumming, girls, then eventually, beers, raving, part-time jobs, money and cars.

Mountain biking faded into the background. I did miss it but there were so many other things going on that I didn't miss it *that* much. Those things were all great fun though, life was good, I was enjoying it and then *BANG!..* Everything changed...

I'd crashed my car... It's a story for another time and another place but it was bad, really bad, tragic... Personally, I was broken in many ways but I'd still been incredibly fortunate. I was alive.

5 - Contradictions and Contrast

Contradictions can be wonderful things. They can take our initial reactions or judgements and turn them completely on their heads. They can transform something we've pegged down as plain or one-dimensional and add new depth or even transform it into a multifaceted dazzling gem!

When it comes to mountain biking, we're already starting off with something awesome. When you throw a leg over, crank those pedals and head out for a session, riding and life seem so simple.

When you take a good hard look at it though, and examine it closely, mountain biking is a glorious, complex bundle of contradictions that make it even more fascinating and even more awesome.

It's not just polarised paradoxes either; there's a vibrant spectrum of contrast from end-to-end and encompassing everything in between.

Let's take physical rider input for example…

Fitness and strength are huge advantages. The fitter and stronger you are, the better you ride. From muscling your rig through rough sections to pumping through the contours of the trail or giving it a big pump and pull for extra air to clear a jump.

There are those heavy landings and big compressions, where you have to muster every ounce of strength to keep your hands on the grips, and to prevent your chest from bouncing painfully off the bars and catapulting you into oblivion.

Sucking up a vicious and unexpected hole, when you're already battling to resist the Gs in a high-speed berm, can take an instantaneous super-human burst of power. Sometimes you've just got to physically muscle your bike to a new line, in the blink of an eye, to get out of trouble or into a sweet spot.

There's sprinting for speed and grinding out climbs. There are times when you need to clamp down your core and your entire upper body, to keep your front wheel down, and to effectively transfer all your pedal input to that small patch of contact at the base of the rear tyre.

It can look like a physical wrestling match to a casual observer and certainly feel like it to us. But whilst all that brute force, physical fitness and raw strength are being applied, there's another section of the orchestra working both in contrast and in complete harmony. There's a section that is playing a role of elegant precision and finesse.

Single fingers on each hand are delicately modulating the brakes, controlling the velocity of all that snarling mass of hurtling momentum. Micro-movements of your whole body are working in unison. Ankles dipping, hips adjusting, body positioning, eyes darting, mind calculating. Everything is adjusting and reacting to keep your head and shoulders quiet and steady like a giant human gimbal.

Every section of the orchestra is contributing to create an exquisite symphony, dancing on the limit of grip, tracking the trail, hitting precise spots of your line at the right speed and the right moment. Everything is perfectly synchronised to maintain optimal flow, prime speed and maximum joy.

The noise, the drama and the physicality of battering over roots, jinking over rocks and juddering over bumps is muted in an instant as you take to the air... All that mayhem dissolves in the *whoomph* of the take-off, leaving silence... Pure calm and total contrast for a fleeting moment, then s*crruuuuff*, back to Earth and the pandemonium returns.

The speed and aggression of descent come as a stark contrast when you abruptly wash off all the speed to delicately pick your way through a technical section or when it's time for quiet contemplation on a climb or sitting on a lift. These moments are a chance for the physical, sensory and reactionary responses to retreat and for your mind to re-emerge to reflect, ponder and plan in peace and calm.

There are ups and downs, literally and figuratively. Highs and lows... Literally and figuratively. Sometimes you're riding like it's a fight to the death and sometimes it's an exquisite dance.

Even the terrain delivers an abundance of contrast. There are rocks and roots and gravel and grit. Then there are muted, fluffy, loamy ribbons of joy, fast grassy meadows, drifty powder dust and squirrelly wet mud.

One minute you can be blowing out of your backside, heart rate blipping off the limiter, sweat pouring out of your body, then the next, you've dialled back into recovery mode, returning to baseline on a lovely, lengthy freewheel descent.

Mountain biking is individual and competitive, yet at the same time collective and collaborative.

You can ride on your own or you can ride with your mates. Even if you don't "officially" compete, there's always a rivalry with your buddies, whether it's unspoken or a source of hearty banter. It's human nature to measure and compare but at the same time, we're helping each other out, supporting progress and progression and working as a unit before, during and after a ride.

The grind, the speed and the onslaught are balanced with the artistry, style and personal flair. Every one of us is riding those trails slightly differently, adding our own unique flavour to the lines, the features and the flow.

Full-face helmets, goggles, dirt, speed, amplitude, noise and danger can all make it seem edgy and intimidating. But what could be more inclusive and inviting than connecting with strangers and riding together, often within minutes of meeting, based purely on a mutual love and shared understanding?

You need perseverance and patience as you build your skill, then commitment and courage when the time comes to push your limits and raise your own bar.

Level-headedness, caution and mental calculation keep you right side up but the tipping point arrives when the next step requires you to hurl all of that out of the window and replace it with faith, courage and commitment.

Force and finesse. Commotion and calm. Risk and reward. Intimidating and inviting. Calculation and commitment. Resilience and resolve. Highs and lows. Competitive and collaborative. Physical and mental.

It's a glorious sport, a multi-faceted gem, a symphony of contrast and contradiction with the layers of an onion and the depths of the ocean. It's an ensemble of exquisite parts and the more you look, the more you find.

6 - Back in the Game

I didn't even go near a bike for a long while after my accident. I physically couldn't at first and then after that, I just didn't. I sustained some significant and permanent injuries, including losing the use of an eye, which meant it might just not be the same. At one point it was uncertain if I'd even walk again, never mind ride.

Anyway, life goes on and I was very grateful just to be alive... Still am.

New things came along and my focus went in different directions. In hindsight, not riding sooner during that time is a bit of a regret but there's no point dwelling on it. You live and learn.

I eventually began dusting off my old rig every once in a while. When I was back home with my folks I'd go and re-ride some of my old favourites and relive some fond memories.

Years later, I ended up on holiday in a place called Fernie in British Columbia, Canada. After seeing riders spilling down the hill and through the bike park, I decided I really fancied a piece of the action and rented a downhill bike for a day...

"*Well hello!...*" That really did reignite my imagination! I hadn't ridden *that* hard for quite a while but I could still do it. It was just like riding a bike, funnily enough, and the bikes had come a long way. They made it even easier and even more fun! I'd never even ridden a bike with suspension before and suddenly I could see the point.

My bikes had never had any suspension, not even in their forks, and I'd merrily clattered over all sorts of terrain. Riding these new, plush rigs that were so comfortable, capable and encouraging was a revelation.

That day in Fernie and the trips down memory lane had re-whet my MTB appetite. I'd had a few tasters and they felt good. For a few years I'd been toying with the idea of getting back into it properly (*"Doo it, doo it, doo it"*) but I'd had enough on my plate and didn't have any biking mates to spur me on… That was until the serendipitous arrival of a new mate in my life which kicked off a marvellous renaissance.

Friends of ours were getting married and the groom-to-be had invited me along on his stag-do to Tallinn in Estonia. He passed on the contact details of another mate of his who was travelling from near where I lived. He suggested we could share a lift to the airport "darn sarf" (down south).

I'd met Baz once before but it had been briefly on a night out and we hadn't really talked much. As soon as we met up though and set off for the airport, we got on like a house on fire. We didn't shut up. Still don't actually. Like a couple of old biddies, we yakked away for the three hours to Gatwick, barely pausing for breath.

We had loads in common and when I mentioned I was thinking about getting back into mountain biking he had just done the same. He'd recently got a bike and had been out a few times but wanted to do way more. "Right!" I said, "As soon as I get home, I'm buying a bike."

Our bromance moved quicker than either of us could have expected… We arrived at the hotel in Tallinn to find that we'd been paired up in a double room. The footprint of the room was occupied almost entirely by the bed. Good job we were getting along because we'd be spending the next few days even closer than either of us could have imagined.

It was an excellent few days though and whilst this is a bit off-topic, one of the highlights was the paint-balling. It was hands-down the best paint-balling I have ever experienced. Absolute total disregard for health and safety. The centre was on an ex-Soviet-era military base. You'd be legging it through the game zone only to have to screech to a halt to avoid falling down an open shaft into an underground bunker or to dodge being torn to shreds by rolls of rusted barbed wire obscured in the undergrowth.

The zone was dotted with derelict buildings of highly questionable structural integrity. That was made worse by the fact that the staff didn't discourage players from clambering up, to take up firing positions on top. We learned in a very short amount of time that there was a high potential for injury if you didn't have your wits about you. That just added to the excitement and dialled the need for mental engagement up to 11!

Anyway, we survived the weekend and Baz and I jabbered all the way back up the M1 at the end of it. We also discovered that we fired up each other's competitive streaks and would definitely be staying in touch.

I got back home and went straight into research mode for a new bike. A couple of weeks later I was the proud owner of a brand-new Giant Trance. It wasn't really the right bike for me in hindsight but I had no idea at the time and it was a start... I was back in the game.

Baz had already been up to Lee Quarry near Bacup to ride a couple of times and as it turned out, it was a perfect meeting point for both of us. We could both get to it in about 45 mins.

At the time, Lee Quarry had enjoyed a cash injection from the local authority and Rowan Sorrell (subsequently, co-founder of Bike Park Wales) and his crew had built a network of trails and skills areas up there which were pretty decent.

The development even extended to a loop over at Cragg Quarry with a long link trail between the two. It was a bit of a slog on the way over but a balls-out, full-charge, fun-fest on the way back. They'd even embedded a bunch of large rocks set at an angle in the ground for some extra "airtime" on the way down.

Lee Quarry was, and probably still is, accessed with a big climb up a track from a tarmac dead-end road at the bottom in Bacup. The road looked like advance infrastructure for some future commercial development but it was a great spot to leave the cars and set off up the hill. There was always talk of a trail centre building or cafe that never seemed to come any closer to fruition.

We'd meet up and get our bikes and kit together before setting off on the big pull up the hill. On the first few rides, I struggled because Baz's bike fitness was way better than mine. It wasn't consciously intentional but I also realised that he kept asking me questions on the climbs. He'd ask a quick question and then settle in for the answer while I waffled on, struggling to get enough oxygen on board between sentences.

I started putting in some overtime, riding and exploring near my home around Halifax and Hebden Bridge. I quickly evened up the fitness levels. I also gave Baz a taste of his own medicine. I turned the tables and got him "blowing out of his arse" with my own line of interview questions. I eventually 'fessed-up and we had a good laugh about it.

Once you made it to the top at Lee Quarry there was plenty to go at. There was a big loop that skirted the top of the open quarry and returned to the top of the access track. The final descent of that loop from the top of the quarry back to the gate was a superb ribbon of delight with plenty of fast rocky challenges, some great jumps and a young wooded section lower down.

There was a black add-on loop at the top dropping down and into the quarry which was paved with large lumps of stone. I snagged a front wheel in the deep joints and OTB'd (over the bars) there on more than one occasion.

There were several smaller loops at the top with fast berms, rollers and jumps. Even more were located within the quarry mouth which were a bit more pedally and technical. There were a few skills areas thrown in too. All in all a fantastic little set up for a weeknight or Saturday morning blast. We had some fantastic times up there and learned a lot.

It could get properly wild up there too. The weather could be insane. One time we were up there and riding the loop skirting the top of the quarry mouth. The wind was howling and we were being pelted with driving rain and hail. The streams were all running high and racing along their beds. Our gaze followed their path as they hurtled towards the edge of the quarry face but rather than plummeting over and into it, they were jetting vertically upwards!

The wind was howling in, up the face of the quarry and shooting the streams of water straight up into the air where they were attempting to leap down into the void. The result was a series of inverted waterfalls jetting vertically into the sky. It was a very cool thing to see. It was also superbly exhilarating and life-affirming to be playing out in those tempestuous conditions.

An added treat on a trip to Bacup was popping into the Rose and Crown in Stacksteads afterwards for a drink, a bite to eat and a post-ride chat. We'd tried a few grotty little pubs around the area before stumbling on this little gem.

An absolutely brilliant pub! The landlord was a big jolly fella who looked like he enjoyed his food and his beer. Don't judge a book by its cover though because this guy was a keen mountain biker and rode all over the place: coast to coasts, trips abroad with his mates, the lot. He was always up for a good chat about riding but he was always busy.

He was busy keeping the place purring. Ticking over like a well-oiled machine. The place was a buzzing community hub whichever night you went. There were quiz nights, carvery nights, karaoke nights and excellent pub grub. He even had a beer garden and a bowling green around the back!

I'd never heard of rag pudding before I went there but I ended up having it most times we went. It was basically like a steak and ale pie but in a delicious suety parcel. A bit like a giant, tasty, gravy-laden, northern dim sum. Delicious! And very welcome after a wild night on the tops.

I don't know if the pub is still the same or if the same bloke still runs it but if you're ever riding over there, it's well worth a visit.

One night was *so* wild though that we were even forced to skip a trip to the Rose and Crown...

Once again, the wind was howling and the rain was driving and it was sheeting down. Immense amounts of water were plummeting from the heavens. From our vantage point on the tops, we could see blue lights strobing all along the valleys below. Fire engines, police cars and ambulances were racing about obviously dealing with a string of 999 emergency calls.

It looked serious so we decided not to hang about too long. We bid our farewells in the parking area and pulled out onto the main road in opposite directions for our drives home…

Well… An attempted drive home for me.

As I drove up and out of Bacup, I was pretty much driving up a riverbed. Water was rushing down the road, carrying rocks, silt and debris, that I was having to dodge on the way. Water was squirting back up out of the storm drain manholes and was even peeling great sheets of tarmac off the pavement from below!

In places, water was being squeezed out from under the ground at high pressure along the back edge of the pavement curb stones. It was shooting several feet in the air in long flat thin fans of water. Quite spectacular.

I made it as far as Todmorden and the road home had been closed. I turned around and went back the way I'd come. I tried to find another way to loop around but that road was now closed too. The police blocking the road said that every road in and out of Todmorden was now impassable. There was no way in or out until the rain stopped and the flooding subsided.

I called my wife Nina to let her know what was happening and that I might have to sleep in the car. I was wet and muddy from riding and didn't fancy a cold night in the car, so I got online and managed to find a bed and breakfast nearby. I rang them up and booked in.

When I got there I discovered I'd got the last available room. The owners were getting busy setting up extra mattresses in the basement for other commuters who'd unexpectedly found themselves trapped on the way home and turned up on the doorstep.

I was very grateful for a great night's sleep, followed by a tasty, bonus, full English breakfast the next morning. Filled contentedly with bacon, eggs and tea, I jumped back in the car and set off home through the debris field, and aftermath of the storm.

My brother decided to get back into riding not long after we did, so we also started meeting up with each other, Baz and other mates to head out for rides. Lee Quarry had kicked things off very nicely and we started searching for more meeting spots nearby to feed the need.

Gisburn, Whinlatter and Grisedale proved handy destinations for us and after reading in a bike magazine that the Howgills boasted one of the longest continuous descents in the UK, we went back there and checked that out. It was well worth it too and the first time we'd ever ridden the far northern side of the range.

First you've got to climb to the top of the Howgill's highest summit, "The Calf" which stands at 676 m. From there though, there's an 11-mile descent all the way back down to where the swell of the fells subside at Bowderdale to the north. The term "continuous descent" may be a touch on the generous side but it wasn't far off and it was a terrific ride.

Uplift was very appealing to us too and Wales became a favourite destination for a big day out or an overnight jolly. Trips to Antur Stiniog and Bike Park Wales with a night in a Welsh pub served as a proper little treat. We even headed up to Fort William for a weekend and rented downhill (DH) rigs to lap the World Cup track and get our first taste of what the top dogs ride.

As the years ticked by, my riding progressed, my skill improved and my love for the sport continued to grow. I knew I wanted to do as much as I could. More trails, more memories, more travels, more progress, more good times and more fun... And, there was a big decision on the horizon that might open up a whole new world of opportunity.

7 - Progression

Mountain biking is an endless journey of progression. We're all on a conveyor belt of progress and if you want to, there's always something to work on or improve.

It could be learning to wheelie, bunny hop or manual. It could be getting fitter to ride further and faster. It could be getting stronger to handle longer descents or gnarlier trails without getting arm pump or fatigue.

It could be learning to jump, to jump further or jump higher. There are step-ups, step-downs, drops, bigger drops and gaps to get to grips with. No two are ever the same. Every feature and every trail is a different learning experience and a new opportunity for progress.

You might want to get faster through flat corners or better at railing berms. You might want to hone your technique and body positioning for optimum grip and maximum speed. You might want to master rock gardens, roots, dirt or dust, wet mud or even snow!

How about schralping? Carrying speed deep into the corner, squaring it abruptly so the rear tyre breaks loose with a crisp-sounding *schralp* and firing a magnificent plume of dust into the air as you accelerate away.

It could be learning to whip, endo, bar-spin or backflip. There are T-bogs, can cans, nac nacs, one-footers, suicide no-handers and no-hander-landers. This is just the tip of an enormous iceberg of tricks and creativity which are only limited by imagination… And imagination is limitless!

There are opportunities for new experiences in cross-country, enduro, slopestyle, downhill or bike park. There's the chance to progress from greens to blues, blues to reds, reds to blacks or blacks to expert. It's always worth taking those classifications with a pinch of salt though. One park's red can be another park's green. Looking at you Châtel.

We can venture away into the wild for freerides, harder freerides or building our own freerides.

There's a whole world of competition opportunities in every discipline and at every stage from local to regional, regional to national, national to continental and continental to world.

We are all on our own paths of progression and whichever particular flavours tickle our taste buds, we're all at the same table and we're all enjoying the same feast.

We are all experiencing the same process of progression. Everybody's been there. We were all beginners once and nobody skipped a step. We all know how it feels to work for and bag another rung of success on the ladder of progress.

The opportunities for progression aren't just limited to riding your bike either. There are so many auxiliary and ancillary aspects to our sport, all of which are ripe for learning and progress. It could be improving maintenance skills, servicing, suspension setup, planning, navigation, first aid, trip management, trail building, feature building, coaching or guiding.

I can't think of a sport with so many directions for progress within such a shared and relatable experience.

It even applies to the trails and lines we ride. It can take years to ride a trail the fastest way, with the best lines. When you've done that, you can switch up the challenge and ride it with maximum "steeze" or creativity as your motivating factor.

I've even got a mate who is a boss-level instructor and bone-fide bike master who now looks for the line that no one else would even dream of riding. Not because it's the fastest, best-looking or most fun but just because it's something different and a new challenge for him.

We're very lucky these days. There are so many resources available to us to aid our journeys of progression. We have access to coaching, tips, techniques and demonstrations at our fingertips. We can watch other people sharing their own progression at all levels, providing motivation and inspiration.

Sometimes opportunities to learn and progress come out of the blue. I had some unexpected breakthroughs a few years ago when I went out with my little lad's bike club... In fact, it was with the same instructor I just mentioned above.

I thought I was just going out to enjoy riding with the kids, to see what they got up to and to pick up any back-markers who might end up in a heap on the floor. A coach is a coach though, and it wasn't long before I was getting some tips too.

He pointed out a couple of flaws in my technique and how I could improve them. I kid you not, those suggestions improved my riding almost instantly. When I have the spare spondoolies, I'll definitely invest in some regular coaching.

We all want different things out of our riding though and some people only want a bit of progress but it's still progression. It's still the same feeling. It's still the same journey and that progression is a huge part of the fun, the reward, the culture and the sport.

8 - A New Life in the Alps

I knew that I wanted to ride as much as possible and we were about to take a leap of faith that looked set to deliver an abundance of new riding opportunities. Funnily enough, one of the key drivers for this next big move was a completely different sport altogether, albeit another one of the gravity-assisted variety.

The seed for this next chapter of our lives was sown way back in that phase when I wasn't even riding bikes. My dad had taken up skiing in his 40s and was immediately hooked. He knew my brother and I had always had a thing for snowboarding and saw an excellent opportunity for some extra father-and-sons good times.

He offered to treat us both to a couple of lessons on the dry slope and then take us away for a holiday. Excellent plan Dad and there was an immediate "Hell yeah!" from the both of us.

We bounced and tumbled our way through a couple of lessons on Penrith dry ski slope, then headed to Val Thorens in the French Alps for our first taste of riding on proper snow. Some bright spark suggested the top of a red run for our first descent. By the time we reached the bottom, we were battered, bruised and totally addicted! Another life-long love affair had begun.

Many, *many* good times followed. We rode the dry slopes in Kendal, Sheffield and Halifax as well as snow domes in

Manchester and Castleford. We headed off for a trip every year, together and with other friends and family.

I got together with Nina a couple of years into it. She already skied but switched to boarding because it was way cooler. (Just kidding skiers, just kidding…) Not only did we share a love of snow and mountains but we enjoyed travelling, moving around, exploring and getting to know new places.

We lived in the US for a year and even managed to squeeze in a winter season snowboarding in Canada a few years later.

We settled in the UK for a while with our feet quietly itching away. We'd give them a good scratch once a year by jumping in the car and driving out to the Alps for a snow fix.

Eventually, we got married, the kids came along and we started them riding bikes and skiing on the dry slope as soon as they were interested. We kept up the winter holidays so that we could share one of our passions and so that they could experience the magic of big mountains and proper winter for themselves.

The dry slope, biking and the annual trips kept those itchy feet at bay for a few years but the idea of another big lifestyle move was always fermenting in the background.

The time was never right, as it seldom is, but as the kids got older and started school, we realised our lives were beginning to crystallise. Getting away was going to become more and more difficult as time went by and probably even more so as they got older. Maybe it was time to roll the dice and give it a go. We could always just go for a bit to try it out and turn around and come back if it didn't work out. It'd be easier to come back than it would be to go.

We weighed up the pros and cons for all of us and started to research where we might go, if we did go. We'd already spent a bit of time snowboarding in the Portes du Soleil. We knew it was a massive and varied area of 12 linked ski stations spanning the French and Swiss border.

The French side made sense because the UK was still in the European Union, so we were legally allowed to turn up in any member state and set up home without the need for a visa, a permit or any significant hassle. Having lived temporarily in the United States and Canada we knew how difficult it could be to get your hands on a residency permit and what a privileged opportunity we had right on our doorstep.

The French side of the Portes du Soleil would also be handy for Geneva and the airport there. Driving home to the North of England within a day was doable. The area was ticking a whole bunch of boxes for us and it could be an amazing experience for the kids.

Ooh, and there was another thing... Most of those ski stations that linked in the winter, also linked in the summer... Together they make up the biggest bike park in Europe, connecting the individually iconic parks of Les Gets, Morzine, Châtel, Avoriaz and Champéry. Hehehehehe!

Whilst I'm at it, I should mention, that to me, snowboarding and mountain biking feel like kindred spirits. They're like brothers from another mother or sisters from another mister. The sensations, culture, mindset, attitude, flow and creativity are very alike and I love 'em both.

Anyway, once we'd weighed it all up, it had to be done. It just seemed like an amazing lifestyle opportunity for all of us individually and for our little family unit. We hoped it would also be one which would spill over to our family and friends.

We whacked our house on the market and it sold straight away. We sold some of our stuff and stuck the rest in storage. We loaded our van with the essentials we'd need for the next few months and set off for France in the middle of winter with a seven year old, a four year old, nowhere to live and no real plans.

We'd hit a snag trying to find a place to live before we set off because long-term rentals appeared to be nigh-on non-existent. Obviously owners could charge top dollar for short-term holiday lets and were understandably less interested in anything else.

We figured, "*Let's just get there and figure it out when we are.*" We did have an insurance policy though. We had some good friends who lived less than a couple of hours away in Switzerland. If it all went to crap we could stay with them while we planned our next move.

We arrived in Les Gets early in February in 2016. We found somewhere to stay for that night and the rest of the week. We then set about looking for something for after that and getting the kids into school. It all seems a bit more "gung-ho" looking back but at the time, it just had to be done and whatever happened, it was an adventure.

We got the kids into the local school, made some new friends, worked online, settled in and set about enjoying the rest of the winter season. There were some big challenges with our leap of faith but all the positives and the adventure of it all were tipping the scales to awesome!

Eventually, the winter started to wane and the weather turned. The snow began to beat a steady retreat up the slopes and toward the higher mountain peaks and the biking possibilities and the trails began to reveal themselves. *Hohohoho!* Here we go!

9 - The Characters

Another cool thing about our grand community of mountain biking compadres is the wide variety of colourful characters. It's always a laugh to 'take the Mickey' and caricature some of the identifiable personality traits.

The following list is wildly stereotypical and by no means exhaustive but here are a few "types" we've probably all come across over the years. In fact, most of us are probably a blend of a few of them to be fair. I know I am.

"The Noob" – Elbows down, weight back, stiff legs and exuding an air of mild panic. At the same time, they are living the freakin' dream! Eyes that should be quickly assessing and moving beyond the next feature are focused firmly on future non-noob riding glory!

"Past-life" – Complete noob who throws a leg over and inexplicably sends it from day one.

"The Test Pilot" – Somebody has to go first and the test pilot is always up for hitting any new feature, gap or drop. After successfully unlocking the level, the floodgates are opened for everyone else.

"Steezy Pete (or Petra)" – Skills to pay the bills and style for days. Everything is a fluid, flowing, fabulous sight to behold.

Touch, technique, balance, flair and sheer artistry with laser precision and cat-like abilities.

"The Funicular" – Climbs like a machine. Rides alone because everyone is sick of the sight of their rear end on the horizon ahead. Resting heart rate 35 bpm.

"Shaun Rider" – Parties all night, sups beers/smokes spliffs all day long but still manages to get the job done astonishingly well. Even more surprisingly, they seem to get it done without catastrophic consequences.

"Captain Caveman" – Wispy beard, bird's nest hair, missing teeth and wild-eyed vacant stare. Was accidentally transported from the Stone Age after stumbling through a time portal in the back of a cave. Emerged in a modern bike park and bumped straight into "Shaun Rider". They immediately got on like a house on fire and the rest is history.

"Gucci" – Impeccable style with new sets of kit every year and always looking sharp. Goes as far as to measure the gap at the base of pants to ensure the correct amount of sock exposure… In their opinion.

"Direct Line" – The fastest route from point A to point B is a straight line. The direct line. No alternatives, no

compromise, no exceptions and no turning, if at all possible. Even better if they can forgo brakes completely. Side effects of the direct line may include making a call to Direct Line insurance when it all goes wrong.

"Bareback Rider" – Less is more. Clothing and protection that is… And potentially skin. Full-face helmet, pants and vest is the current dress code although completely shirtless is becoming popular. Half expecting to see someone sending it in just a full-face helmet and speedos sometime soon.

"Anal Compulsive Disorder" – Everything just so… Bike is spotless and serviced to perfection 30 minutes after returning from a ride. Garage workshop is shelved out with a full set of every spare imaginable, labelled and ready to go. I just found out that the French word for someone like this is "maniaque" which translates as maniac… Hmm, veeeery interesting.

"Cautious Carl" – Knows the chicken runs like the back of their hand. Pushes downhill from time to time. Caution is a good thing in general, it keeps you the right way up but sometimes commitment must prevail.

"The Gobshite" – Offends everyone. "Those bikes are totally overpriced for what you get." "Aren't you supposed to be good to ride one of those?" The Gobshite mistakenly

believes they are engaging in witty, ice-breaking banter. This is not necessarily how it is being interpreted by the recipient. How they've made it this far and retained a full set of teeth is a complete mystery.

"Full Send" – Always on it. Dawn 'til dusk. First run to the very last, no change in pace, no change in commitment, just a constant, consistent level of full send.

"Loose Dog" – Some people just let it all hang out and dance (maybe mosh) on the edge of reason. It shouldn't work but it does and how the heck do they get away with it?

"The Shralpaholic" – Making a turn without schralping has become a physical impossibility. Berms quake on their approach and are left destroyed in their wake. Shapers are setting up Shralpaholic's Anonymous meetings to curb the epidemic and safeguard their workmanship.

"Jerry of the Day" – This can be any one of us at any time and it can strike completely out of the blue. No-one is exempt from a bout of numpty-ness once in a while. Must be captured on camera to truly qualify.

"The Smart Arse" – It's not always a question but you always get an answer, sometimes an hour-long "Ted Talk".

Specialist chosen subject... Everything! Technique, maintenance, setup, navigation, trails, you name it.

"The Oracle" – The actual font of mountain bike knowledge. Happy to share but nothing to prove. Answers to your questions are succinct, delivered with humility and tact.

"Yoda" – A true bike master, often found deep in the woods. Mythical bike-ability and the source of legendary tales. Usually a little funny looking due to the amount of time spent deep in the forest. The line that nobody else takes/sees/dares to take/would dream of taking... That's the line. Often found imparting bike wisdom to younger generations.

"Flash" – Slow-mo to woah-bro!.. In normal life they are so laid back, they are almost horizontal. Like the sloth from Zootopia they are mega chill until it's time to ride and the beast is unleashed!

"The Jack Russell" – High energy, uber-competitive and always yapping at your back wheel. Doesn't want to be left behind or miss out on doing anything you do. Has "Anything you can do I can do better" running on a loop inside their head while riding.

"The Tool" – Thankfully, these are few and far between but they do roll among us. Can usually be found terrorising slow noobs or riding by on the other side.

"Omitakaya" – At "one" with the forest. Expert trackers and freeride trail guides.

"Billy Big Bollocks" – Will send anything in their path. Limits?.. What limits? Boundaries?.. What boundaries? "Let's just give it a go and see what happens."

"Emilia Earhart" – Explorer extraordinaire. "I'm 100% sure it's this way." Gets lost every time.

"The Racer" – Whether they race, raced or should have raced, they are just straight-up rapid!

"Highlander" – Immortal and indestructible. These guys can take a beating. They walk away from major offs and cataclysmic events with barely a scratch. "There can be only one!"

"La Cucaracha" – As above.

"The Surgeon" – Dissects trail details with the precision of a brain surgeon. A regular human would need to undertake a six-year degree and four years of clinical training to achieve

similar levels of anatomical trail knowledge. Scalpels for tyres, incising the intricate trail features with nano-metric accuracy.

"The Grig" – That's Greg, pronounced in a South African accent, as in Minnaar. This refers to the eternal youthful Peter Pan-like qualities of the current GOAT. Interestingly, mountain biking itself is in fact the secret elixir of eternal youth so there are ever-growing numbers of age-defying rippers. If the wider population catches on we'll have an exacerbated overpopulation crisis on our hands.

10 - First Summer in the Alps

I'd been to a few bike parks in the UK and had great times but I had never ridden *anywhere* on the continent. I was super excited about what our new home had in store. The scale, diversity and accessibility of what was about to unfold was tantalising.

Like a prototype car being unveiled at the Geneva Motor Show just up the road, nature gradually pulled back the snowy white dust sheet of winter. First, it revealed the troughs of the valleys, then the gentle slopes and finally the high mountain peaks. Snow was on the wane and dirt was on the rise!

Summer was fast approaching and the promise of five linked bike parks, 12 resort towns, 22 lifts, 600 km of official trails and goodness knows how many kilometres of unofficial trails, was literally making my mouth water. The towns would soon be bubbling with fellow riders, bikes, bike shops galore and a top-notch MTB atmosphere. Get in!

The bike lifts normally open for a couple of early weekends each year, before opening permanently from mid-June until early September. That meant I had several weeks to build some bike fitness before it'd be game on!

The kids were excited too. They had loved the winter and were open to trying anything that might be anywhere near as fun. Even Nina was up for it despite her mountain bike career consisting solely of that one day of downhill in Canada.

We made a whistle-stop tour back to the UK to visit family and friends, then we picked up our bikes from storage, turned around and gunned it back across France.

Let the exploration begin!

And holy moly!.. The climbs were an immediate shock to the system. If I'd thought the first slog back at Bacup was a wakener, these were like Lee Quarry on steroids. It just seemed like everything was a serious climb, followed by a descent that seemed to be over way too soon, and then yet another lung-busting climb.

My fitness soon started to build though. It's funny how even when you've got a reasonable base level of fitness, it still takes two or three weeks to start feeling fit when you switch focus from one sport or physical activity to another. I guess it's the same with your brain and mental applications actually.

Anyway, there was no way I'd be convincing Nina or two young kids to accompany me on those climbs, so for the time being, if we wanted a family ride, we went and played down at the Dérêches in Morzine. It's a wooded area following the banks of the Dranse river. It's popular with dog walkers and is one of the few level-ish places nearby to ride with the family. Watch out for dog poo though.

Luckily, the top of quite a few bike trails in the area are accessible by road, so we could even add in a few shuttle runs with the van. We'd chuck the bikes in the back for a bit of uplift-assisted downhill action. The kids approved!

As the snow disappeared the trail crews and shapers got to work with mini-diggers and hand tools, repairing and redesigning sections of trail. They'd tart up the sections that had been hibernating under the snow and rebuild others that had been completely levelled to make way for a nice, level ski piste in the winter.

This year though, there was another trail-building crew in town. A big one, with big toys and a big budget which they were using to build some monster features.

If I wasn't already excited enough about the impending season, I was getting whipped into even more of a frenzy because Crankworx was coming to Les Gets, for the first time ever.

Crankworx is a gravity-fed competitive mountain bike tour. It'd be stopping at three venues that year. First would be Rotorua in New Zealand, then Les Gets and then on to Whistler in Canada where the whole thing had been conceived.

We would be treated to a week-long festival of mountain bike competition. There'd be a huge slopestyle course, a downhill competition, dual speed and style, dual-slalom, pump-track and whip-offs. Some of the best riders in the world would be visiting and putting their skills on show in the hope of bagging prize money, exposure and kudos.

Before the riders could do their thing, the courses and infrastructure for the event needed to be in place. The Crankworx crew got to work and a yellow fleet of super-sized, off-road earth-moving trucks roared into action, shipping in tons of soil for the slopestyle course. The jumps rose steadily from the Earth, reaching spectacularly towards the heavens like giant termite mounds. A chorus of chainsaws revved into life and got busy sculpting wood structures for the start gantry, drops, and giant whale tail on-off ramp.

The clock kept counting down towards Crankworx and the lifts opening. I kept riding, getting fitter and sharper with a background fuzz of increasing excitement.

And suddenly it all kicked off! The lifts opened in early June and I was practically camped out, ready and waiting to get on the first one.

Riding a chairlift has always been a pleasure. An excellent and underused means of transportation in my opinion. You're outside, seated and elevated for great views. It's a great place to think, reflect, zone out or have a chat. Love it!

Riding the Chavannes Express chair was already firmly associated with many good times from the winter and riding it in summer, with my bike on board, was a massive treat!

I parked my backside on the vinyl-coated cover of the six-seater chair and sailed up, up and away out of the base station. Good times and thrills beckoned ahead. The chairs in front whirred steadily up the hill, funnelling between the banks of pine trees on either side as they led the way.

Away to the left, the deck chairs and parasols of L'Aprèski Bar came into view, ready and waiting to greet legions of thirsty punters as they'd funnel back throughout the day. The timber-clad structures of Les Gets multiplied in the distance as my vantage point rose and my field of view expanded.

The church spire projected above the mass and drew my gaze for a moment before my focus was pulled onwards to the ever-spectacular spectre of Pointe de Nantaux beyond, its triangular bulk standing tall, proud and perfectly framed by the V of the Les Gets col.

The giant Crankworx features scrolled past, beneath my free-swinging feet. There was already a bustle of activity underway as the final preparations and finishing touches were being made.

The chair chugged on, leaving the noise and commotion behind, pulling steadily on, up into the quiet calm of the trees and the mountains above.

I spent the next few hours blatting all over the place and exploring everything the bike park on the Chavannes side had to offer... Well... Everything my skill level would allow.

Sensibly, I started on the greens before moving on to the blues and reds. It was sloppy and wet but already awesome fun. I could see I was going to need to improve my technique to get the most out of it though. The conditions were already making it difficult to get up to "trail speed" in many sections. I could see that even if it was bone dry, I'd probably be struggling to maintain enough speed in some places.

At the time, there were quite a few sections with multiple tight berms and table-tops between them. Carrying enough speed through the berms to clear the table and maintain speed for the next berm and the next table was something I wasn't used to. It was going to need some work. I'd need to get to know the trails, figure out the best lines and develop better berm-cornering technique to ride these things like they were designed to be ridden.

All-in-all though, I was over the moon. This was going to be epic. I'd already spent more time riding downhill in a single day than I had the rest of the year.

I made my final descent and joined the queue of mud-splattered riders at the bike wash. I sprayed my bike, and myself, down and met Nina and the kids at the Aprèski for a well-earned post-ride beverage.

The season was underway! I was underway and one week later, Crankworx was underway!

Despite the weather's best efforts to derail it, Crankworx delivered! It opened with a big "whip off" competition, on a mega-kicker behind the tourist office and barrelled straight into several days of nutty bike skills and mind-blowing riding.

There was so much to watch and so much to see, with a packed calendar of varied events. Even when the finals of the events aren't on, there are practice sessions, qualifying, brand stands, signings, the pits and all sorts.

So many legends and pros from the various disciplines of the sport mooching around town at the same time was kind of trippy. You could walk down the street past the likes of Brett Tippee, Kyle Strait, Jill Kintner, Fabien Barel, Casey Brown and Nicholi Rogatkin in a matter of minutes.

The organisers rattled through the dual-slalom, speed-and-style and pump track challenge while the weather window was still good. Local team P2V even hosted a mini-bike challenge for all-comers on 20" wheeled kids' bikes. It was crackers! Riders were sending it down some of the dual speed and style course followed by one of the big ramps of the slopestyle course. There were some pretty big crashes on this one but thankfully everyone got up and walked away.

As the week went on, the weather got worse. So bad unfortunately that they ended up having to cancel the Slopestyle. This is really the defining event for the Crankworx series but it was deemed unsafe for the riders to proceed and a wise call.

They replaced it with a best trick competition on the final kicker and Nicholi Rogatkin took the title with his infamous "twister" 1080 spin. He nailed it after coming up short on an earlier attempt and spectacularly landing on the lip of the landing.

There was no stopping the downhill though. The wetter the better... Well, that's not strictly correct but it's still fun... The downhill races were set to close-out proceedings on the Sunday and as expected it was a slop-fest of deep mud and wet conditions on Mont Chéry. It was a great atmosphere though and a terrific spectacle from the riders. Frenchies Rémi Thirion and Morgane Charre took the top steps.

It was a shame about the weather but it had been a super-cool week nonetheless. Les Gets had delivered on its return to hosting on the big stage of elite-level mountain biking and Crankworx was booked in to return for the next two years.

OK, bear with me for a moment... I'm just going to do a quick rewind to several days earlier in the week. We'd been hanging out watching the mini bike challenge and had bumped into one of the other mums from school.

Towards the tail end of winter, we'd met her in Le Boomerang. Le Boomerang is an Aussie/French bar, restaurant (and hotel at the time) with its own fair share of connections and stories in mountain bike folklore.

As we'd chatted and got to know each other she said "D'you know what? You and my partner would get on like a house on fire. He loves snowboarding, downhill mountain biking and loads of other mad stuff. I can't wait for you to meet him!"

Well, it had been a couple of months since that conversation and I hadn't met him. I had seen her a few times though and every time she'd say, "Oh man. I can't wait for you to meet Jacko."

The pressure had been building for us to get along. There was potential for a slightly awkward encounter if we met and there was zero chemistry. We were about to find out though because he was due to arrive and meet her any second now! It felt like a blind date all of a sudden but when he turned up, we did indeed get on like a house on fire.

We hung out for the rest of the day and moved with the crowd to continue the party at Barbylone later on. We rabbited away about a whole ton of common interests. At the end of the night, we swapped numbers, parted ways and arranged to meet for a ride.

I was excited but nervous. By the sounds of it, he was obviously happy sending much bigger stuff than I was. I'd be needing to fish my big boy pants out for the occasion.

We met up a few days later and it was mint! We blatted around Les Gets and Morzine, down many of the trails I'd explored a little bit already and then down a whole bunch of "secret" freeride trails that I hadn't even noticed.

We'd veer off the beaten path and drop into secluded strips of single-track, then pop out again somewhere totally unexpected, then back in and out again somewhere else. Some of them were so steep, you couldn't even come to a complete perpendicular stop. If you came off, which I did, you'd just keep sliding, with a bike wrapped in your legs, sometimes face first.

He took me down the blacks at the top of the Nauchets lift and showed off by sending many of the big gaps and features. I followed, clumsily slipping and sliding down into the troughs of each one and scrabbling back up and out of the other sides again.

He was definitely comfortable sending bigger stuff than me and he was rapid down those steep freerides in the woods. I *was* close enough on most stuff though. I was already improving and enthusiastic enough for us to be good riding companions.

The next couple of months were awesome! Jacko's insatiable appetite to ride was matched by my own and he took great pleasure in showing me around and sharing his passion and knowledge. I thought I was getting special treatment and that he was enamoured by my glittering personality, sense of humour and bike riding potential but it turns out he's pretty much like that with everyone.

He'll strike up a friendship with anyone who shows even the slightest interest in riding a bike, or a snowboard, or skis, or a speed-wing, or a motorbike. I was having a great time hanging out and riding together though and I was keen as mustard to sponge up any bit of information and experience I could. Our enthusiasm and the fact we did get along meant it was game on!

We went all over the place and we went everywhere at full pelt. We spent bags of time in Les Gets and Morzine, quite a bit in Super Morzine and Avoriaz and more time in Châtel that year than I have in any season since. All the hopes and anticipation of what was to come had manifested into reality and it was fantastic.

As the seasons gradually rotated, the drab brown of the wet spring dried out and gave way to the brilliant greenery of the woodland. The mountain meadows were airbrushed with sprays of colour from alpine wildflowers. The mountains took on a whole new character as the profusion of life bloomed on their flanks.

The final pockets of snow slowly surrendered to the strength of the summer sun and the area began teeming with riders, hikers, insects and birds. The whole hive of activity playing out to a soundtrack of cowbells and mountain streams.

Each bike park delivered its own individual character. Some days you fancied one, some days another and some days several.

I followed Jacko down so many blacks, freerides and sketchy things that summer that my butthole was in an almost constant state of perma-pucker. He's great but he's not the best at giving you a heads-up on what's coming up. I'd regularly end up unexpectedly on a super-steep rocky section, a suspended northshore rope bridge without any sides, or a narrow elevated balance board without any pre-warning. That did make me realise though, that reactive riding is actually a strong point for me and that gave me even more confidence to just keep going for it.

That first summer was awesome (although, they all have been to be fair)… I rode loads! I rode on my own, I rode with Jacko, I rode with Nina, I rode with the kids. Thomas was hooked straight away and absolutely loved it. He lapped up the reaction he got in the bike park as everyone cheered on this little dude with a full-face helmet, doing his best to send it with the big guys. He was on an Islabike at the time with V brakes and zero suspension but he was "blasting" down the trails with no fear and maximum excitement.

I also rode with other friends we'd met. Some of them were part-time mountain bikers really. They loved it, but it was more of an occasional activity when they fancied a break from the things that really floated their boats. One of those mates is a keen road biker first and foremost but he suggested we head out for my first mountain bike loop of the Portes du Soleil.

I knew he cranked out some serious kilometres on the tarmac and I knew there'd be a fair bit of peddling and climbing to complete the circuit. I was quietly concerned about my ability to keep up and how wrecked I might be at the end of the day.

We rode out from Les Gets across to Morzine then up and over the Super Morzine area towards Avoriaz before diving down into the gorgeous Lindarets valley.

From there, we whirred up the Chaux Fleurie lift before diving down to Pierre Longue and skirting round to Châtel. The Super Châtel shuttle hauled us up high and we climbed even higher on the bikes ready to drop down to Morgins. A lovely loamy woodland descent took us down into the town and a rickety chair ride chugged us up the other side. Reaching the top gave us our first peep of the day into the stunning Champéry valley.

It was up here where we experienced the highlight of that day. A moment that is branded into my memory was riding a cinematic section of single-track skirting a ridge in a juicy green alpine meadow, high above Morgins. The stunning ridge line of the Dents du Midi across the valley to our left, blue skies overhead and not a soul in sight. It was such an astonishingly idyllic mountain biking scene and peak moment to be living, that I almost had to pinch myself.

We picked and pedalled our way round the Swiss boundary of the Portes du Soleil, from Morgins to Champoussin and on to Les Crosets. We hitched the Mossettes lift back to the Swiss/French border, ready for the long descent back into Lindarets and the return journey to Les Gets.

I needn't have worried about my fitness as it turned out. I held my own (ish) and I was obviously much fitter than I'd realised.

It was a fabulous day out and many thanks to me ol' mate Chris for leading the way.

What a summer!

So many experiences and so many memories. I learned loads that season and my progression accelerated exponentially.

I even developed a little personal speed challenge where I'd go "hunting". I'd let random strangers drop into a trail, give them a little while to get ahead before dropping in after them and trying to reel 'em in! Great fun and I still do it actually.

I have since learned that pushing too hard to catch someone, or even pushing too hard when riding with others, is not always the best idea though. The level around here is very high. A lot of world-class riders choose to spend their down time in the area. They, their mechanics, entourages, the locals and even the local youngsters can be insanely rapid. I've got much better at gauging when to charge and when to check my ego at the door and stand down. It's not an exact science though and will probably forever be a work in progress.

I did fall off quite a bit that first summer and I left a fair bit of my skin and DNA lying around the Portes du Soleil. I constantly found myself questioning my comfort zone, where my limits were and how hard I could push to progress.

I was riding my Kona Process 153 that I'd bought in the UK. It was a great bike but I was asking quite a lot of it. I was racing around, trying to stay on the back wheel of Jacko on his downhill weapon. That bike took a beating and I spent a wad on spares and repairs that year.

For some reason, I always seemed to snap the chain or wreck a derailleur a long way from home in Châtel. But every cloud has a silver lining and those mishaps allowed me to discover the joys of riding chain-less. First of all, the peace and quiet without the chain and derailleur slapping around is a blissful pleasure. Secondly, the improvement in my riding that came from trying to hold and generate speed along the trail without the luxury of a few pedal strokes was significant.

The Kona had stood me in good stead though and it had forced me to improve where I might not have done if I'd jumped straight on a DH rig. I'd got a season under my belt now though and I wanted to try a big bike. As luck would have it one of the bike rental shops was selling its fleet of Giant Glorys for what looked like a reasonable price. They were only one season old and had been fully refurbished to sell on. "*Doo it, doo it*" added buying one to its repertoire.

And then, all of a sudden, it was all over. The lifts closed and the season came to an end. It was as if a switch had been flipped and the last visitor out of town had knocked the power off on their way out.

It's a strange feeling that happens at the end of every season but we're used to it now. In fact, the contrast is becoming a little less as more people have begun to visit in

73

between seasons. It's become more of a fading transition than a sudden shift.

I still went riding, pedalled a bit and did the odd shuttle run but for the most part, we were on the approach to winter. The bikes would eventually be cleaned, lubed up and packed away, ready for next year.

Our move to France had been a big one and that first summer had been awesome! I really appreciate all the people who did and still do ride with me and show me new stuff. Exploring the diverse riding opportunities, scenery and trails and feeling my riding progress was and is amazing.

I feel the need to insert a little caveat here. I've been waxing lyrical about our move to the mountains and it can look and sound like an idyllic bed of roses but it hasn't been without its challenges. There have been many sacrifices, compromises and disappointments, both foreseen and totally unexpected. It's not been easy from time to time but there's no point in dwelling on the negatives. Having said that, even if we went back with the benefit of hindsight we'd definitely make the same decision.

11 - Planning and Preparation

Hands up who used to put their homework off until the last minute?.. Me!.. I would imagine a decent number of you guys did too, or maybe still do.

I even used to play 'Return Roulette' with my self-assessment tax return and see how late I could leave it to complete and submit before the deadline. I've been within single-digit minutes. It always felt like I was sticking it to the man a little bit, without actually sticking it to the man at all, or actually getting in any trouble… "*Wuss!*" In fact, I don't even mind paying tax in principle, as long as it's levied fairly, put to good use and not mismanaged, misappropriated or squandered… "*Ahem!*" *side eyes towards powers that be and clears throat*

Anyway… Mountain biking ain't homework and it sure as heck ain't tax returns!

The British Army coined a phrase known as the 7Ps which goes, "Proper Planning and Preparation Prevents Piss Poor Performance". An excellent adage to live by and highly applicable for us mountain bikers. Applicable first and foremost, when it comes to our bikes.

A properly functioning, well-tuned rig cannot only be the difference between a safe, drama-free ride and calamitous disaster but it can also be the difference between a regular ride and a confidence-inspired, limit-pushing, send-session!

I'd be lying if I said I skip merrily along every time I need to get everything prepped. Sometimes I can't be arsed but d'you know what?.. I pretty much always end up enjoying myself when I'm doing it and it always feels great to be properly prepared. It's awesome when your bike is purring like a kitten and ripping like a dream.

Hanging out in the garage usually ends up being an enjoyable experience. Tunes on, mug of coffee or a beer on the go, the smell of WD40 in the air, tools and grease all over the lid of the chest freezer. Checking everything over. Ticking off the mental list of items. The dull ache of oil-engrained and well-worked hands afterwards. I hate to admit it but on some level, I even like the dank smell of stale tyre air!

Before every ride, a quick once over is always a sensible move. Checking all the bolts are tight, tyre pressures, brake pads, hoses, spokes, dropper, suspension and gears.

Lube applied, helmet polished, protection on, nuts tightened and away we go!

Sometimes, there's a bit of extra bike prep needed. Sometimes there are repairs to make, replacements to do or longer-term servicing items. Some of these can require a bit more leg work. We might need to shop around to get the right thing at the right price and then wait for it to arrive if we ordered it online.

We might need to pour over YouTube vids to learn how to replace and tune. Luckily, there are buckets of info out there nowadays, both from manufacturers and other riders to help us with almost everything.

Sometimes though, we haven't got the time, inclination or skills to do it ourselves. When that happens, we need the pros (*God bless 'em! And thank you all*) and like a dentist or a barber, when we find a good one, we are *golden*. Some things are even more specialised like suspension servicing and setup. If you are ever in Les Gets, my mate at Jaff VTT is the man for the job! Boss-level suspension guru and "*direct line*" specialist to boot.

In addition to our bikes, there can be a whole bunch of other things to prep, depending on where we're riding, how we are riding and for how long.

There's the usual: phone, money, spares, tools, water, kit, bike, protection, suncream, snacks, physical and mental fitness.

If you're riding in the bike park, you might be able to get away with very little. The risk of having to walk your bike off the hill if you get a problem can be worth it for the extra freedom of riding super-light.

It's still worth taking everything you might need and leaving it nearby in the van or car, just in case. It's also worth checking the weather, opening times, routes and whether or not you can grab something to eat somewhere.

Longer XC or enduro-style rides like a trip around the Portes du Soleil usually require a bit more planning and preparation. It might be worth taking a pack with water, snacks, first-aid kit, spares, pump, map, chain-link, spare gear cable, mech hanger, pump, gas, tube, tool, extra layer, raincoat and cable ties.

In fact, let's just pause for a moment of reflection and gratitude for the humble cable tie. What an invention! One of the most versatile and useful items in our arsenal and it's responsible for saving the day on countless occasions. They even give you the pleasure of salvaging other people's rides. I've lost count of the number of times I've heard, "Excuse me pal. You haven't got a cable tie by any chance have you?"

We might need to make even more arrangements for a bigger trip away or to go racing. Things like additional insurance, accommodation, travel arrangements or race rubber. We might be riding with a mixed group and need to plan ahead to take ability and fitness into account.

I've got my eye on a couple of big-league, multi-day rides like the Haute Route from Chamonix Mont Blanc to Zermatt and I've literally just read about another from Chamonix to Briançon which sounds cool. These rides look amazing and will no doubt need some planning and preparation items that I haven't even considered before.

There are a shedload of possibilities and permutations for what we need to prep to ride and it's always useful to remember that proper planning and preparation prevents piss poor performance.

We're not just a ragtag band of adrenaline junkies after all but a damn well organised bunch of planners and project managers. We've got a whole load of stuff to keep organised even if we don't realise it.

12 - Pass'Portes Du Soleil

There's an annual event in the Portes du Soleil called the Pass'Portes du Soleil. *See what they did there?* It's a well-known event and people come from all over the place to take part.

Now, I'd never heard of it before we moved out here but plenty of people back in the UK had apparently. A few of them had also informed me that it's one of the best days out they've ever had on a mountain bike. *High praise indeed.*

I watched for a few years as muddy, fatigued but happy-looking riders streamed around the Portes du Soleil. They'd shovel in local goodies at the various food stations and wash them down with a cold beer here and there. *"Looks like fun."* I thought.

If you've not heard of it before either, the Pass'Portes du Soleil is a lift-assisted mountain bike tour of the Portes du Soleil area which straddles the Franco/Swiss border. The event encompasses the resorts of Les Gets, Morzine, Avoriaz, Châtel, Les Lindarets-Montriond, Champéry, Les Crosets, Morgins and Torgon. It usually acts as a season opener for the full Portes du Soleil mountain bike lift network.

This tour is not dissimilar in principle to the one I did with Chris but it's much more extensive. Extra sections are opened, extra lifts to access more areas and there's obviously the buzz of being part of a major event. This year, it looped in the opposite direction to the one Chris and I had taken and was going to be different again.

During the Pass'Portes, riders cover 80 km in a single day, with 6000 m of vertical ascent (lift-assisted) and 6000 m of descent (gravity-assisted). There are numerous food stations to refuel participants with the different local specialities of each town.

The event runs for three days, over Friday, Saturday and Sunday. Entrants book tickets for their chosen day and to depart from a specific town on the course. A percentage of tickets are allocated to each departure town in order to stagger the starts and balance the flow of traffic around the circuit.

There are even a number of special "options" around the route where you can dip into more challenging downhill sections if you fancy it.

Tickets are known to fly off the shelves like hotcakes. Having decided that I fancied giving it a go, I hit up a few mates to see if they were interested in joining me. After a few messages, I'd lined up an Englishman, an Australian and a Frenchman (insert your own joke).

I readied myself at the keyboard on release day to book our tickets for Saturday. The bookings opened and I filled out one application, no problem. By the time I went to enter the second name, it had sold out for Les Gets on Saturday! *"What the actual?!"*

I quickly cancelled the first application and tried again for all of us on Sunday. "*Result!*" We were in! My French mate swiftly mentioned it to a couple of his French mates and they managed to get in, too. We'd be turning out a six-man international squad.

The previous two years had been a ming-fest weather-wise but as our Pass'Portes weekend beckoned, it looked like we were on for a belter of a day!

The lifts open earlier in the morning for the event, so we all met at the Les Gets tourist office at 7.30 am on Sunday to collect our event packs. We collected our passes, number plates, and goodie bags from the welcome desk. The bags contained some bumph which I never ever got round to reading, a mini tin of WD40 and a very decent waterproof jacket which has lasted extremely well, and I still use to this day.

We got all our kit together and pedalled over to the Chavannes Express lift, loaded our bikes and settled in for the ride to the top in the sunshine. The AprèSki Bar appeared away to the left and was already looking inviting as we rose up and out of the lift station. A relaxing refreshment there would have to wait until we'd got 80 km and a full day's riding under our belts. We offloaded at the top, saddled up and set off on our first section towards the Les Gets golf course.

Aussie Mick led the way. He'd done it before and he's quick. Jacko and I alternated in second and third and the

Frenchies brought up the rear. The three of us were already riding regularly but the French lads hadn't spent as much time on their bikes in recent years. That's definitely changed in the years since though. They now regularly pop up on my Instagram feed doing all sorts of fun-looking MTB-related (or "VTT" as they say in French) stuff.

It was still early as we started the climb to the golf course but it was already turning into a seriously hot day. One of our new French mates was used to his bikes having a bit more horsepower and well, a petrol engine. It quickly became clear that he'd be sleeping very well at the end of the day! If not before it.

We finished the climb and caught our breath, freewheeling down the track to the top of Morzine's Pleney lift. From here the route would follow the blue "Family" trail looping away to the north and back around to the base of the Pleney.

This was our first proper descent of the day. There'd been a lot of chat about: "Just taking it steady", "not pushing it too hard" and "not fully fit…" Needless to say, we set off at Mach 10! Not steady in the slightest, pushing to the limit and not a thought for sub-prime fitness levels. The pace meant it wasn't long at all before we popped out of the woods, grinning manically for the last stretch into Morzine.

We pedalled across town, accompanied by an ever-growing stream of fellow riders and hit our first bottleneck. The Super Morzine bubble lift. There was already a lengthy queue. Thankfully it only took about 20 minutes to clear which wasn't too painful.

We'd arranged to meet another Brit mate there who was joining us for the day and we went through a bunch of FrAnglaise introductions with the rest of the crew.

We rode the bubble lift up to the top, then jumped straight onto the Zore chairlift. The Zore sails over the Super Morzine bike park. It's always a great vantage point to check out the trails and watch fellow riders ripping their way down. If you're lucky, you'll get a few lads or lasses hitting the massive "widow-maker" kicker just beneath and throwing big whips to please the captive audience on the lift above.

On a hot day like that one, sitting in the fresh air was a welcome contrast to the stuffy confines of the Super M bubble. As the lift climbed, Pointe de Ressachaux reared up to the right and a spectrum of greens from juicy meadows to deep dark woodland collided with the vivid blue of the perfectly clear sky above and beyond the ridged horizon.

Disembarking at the top, we set off on the long track through woodland on the wide shoulder that stretches up to the Avoriaz plateau. We popped out at the junction where the Avoriaz road forks down to Lindarets. Here, we peeled off left into the undergrowth for our own descent into the Lindarets valley. This is a long, natural and fun descent. It winds through the bracken and woodland, picking its way over strange formations of dissolved limestone bedrock, jagged and uneven but polished smooth with exposure. We'd normally bank left again halfway down and head towards Châtel but the route for today was leading us straight towards the bottom of the Mossettes lift… And another big queue!

It was only about 10.30 am by now and it was already reading 38°C on the lift station temperature display. Yeah, it was definitely hot but it can't have been *that* hot. I'm sure the thermometer must have been overdue for a calibration check-up.

We nudged along in the queue before boarding and floating up the line of the Mossettes lift. We cruised up over the border line with Switzerland and on to the highest point of the whole tour. We scuttled off just below the summit of Pointe de Mossettes at 2,250 m and paused for a moment to take in the magnificent views back towards Morzine, Les Gets and Avoriaz and behind to the spectacular Dents du Midi ridge towering above Champéry.

We grabbed a few group photos and then got back on it, starting the descent further into Switzerland and down towards Champéry. The heat, the queues, a big group with a range of fitness levels meant we weren't making terrific time. It was becoming clear that if we were going to do the whole thing, we'd need to crack on.

There were a lot of gravely fire roads with drifty corners on the descent from Mossettes. Our competitive natures kicked in and we started charging hard, jockeying for position and diving around each other to keep switching up the lead. We dipped off the tracks and onto some rocky paths through the woods before some road sections to finish. We'd covered almost 1000 m of descent in one blurry, high-speed hit.

The collection of gazebos, tables and benches forming the food station in Champéry coaxed us in. We shovelled in cheese, dried meats, bread, raclette, potatoes, pickles, fruit and chocolate. We washed it all down with cordial and fizzy pop. I'm not sure if it's a combination conducive to peak physical performance but it tasted great and it gave us a chance for a proper group chat.

The big cable car hauled us out of Champéry and we rallied and railed our way down the super fun red downhill section into Les Crosets. It was back up to Mossettes from the Swiss side now before another lengthy descent out towards Morgins. More dusty, gravely tracks and sharp switchbacks proved great fun as we all tanked-on before hauling on the breaks and drifting and sliding through the corners. The unofficial four-cross (seven-cross) competition resumed with everyone overtaking, undertaking and dancing on the limit to try and take or keep the lead.

There was another climb back out of Morgins in Switzerland and over the pass before crossing back into France and descending through the woods into Châtel.

Everyone was boiling hot, soaked with sweat, caked with dust and ready for another food stop. The food court here was set up near the lake at the top of town and fat French "diots" (local Savoie sausages) were on the specialty list this time.

The afternoon was getting on now and it looked like doing the full 2hr30ish Torgon loop, just to arrive back at this point, might be a step too far. We had a debate about just heading straight to the bike park in Châtel and doing some downhill laps instead. This was a popular option but somehow we agreed on doing as much of the Torgon loop as we could squeeze in.

It was time for the first mechanical pitstop of the day and it was mine. As I pulled my bike up to get going again I noticed I'd got a flat. "*Dammit!*" A quick tube change and we headed off to the Super Châtel bubble lift. From there it was onwards and upwards towards Torgon. I'm super-glad we opted to do this section because it was brand new territory for me in the summer and the scenery was different again. We were rewarded with some lovely single-track through lush, green, high mountain pastures.

We eventually made our way back to the bottom of the Super Châtel lift and settled in for by far the most challenging part of the day. It was roasting hot by now, we were fatigued and we had about 6 km of inclined pedal all the way out to the Pierre Longue area of Châtel. We lost a lot of time here because we were struggling with the heat and hydration. Good fortune shone on us though as we rounded a corner and saw an oasis up ahead.

There are a scattering of water troughs throughout the Alps. They typically consist of a log, split longways, hollowed-out and laid flat to form a trough. Another smaller timber branch is connected at one end standing vertically. This piece has been cored out with a water pipe pulled through it. One end is fed to a nearby spring or watercourse and the other provides a constant stream of fresh water, cascading from the vertical member and keeping the trough filled to the brim.

Drinking from the trough would definitely be hazardous to health as I assume it's designed for goats and cows but the locals get stuck into the supply from the hose and if it's good enough for them, it's good enough for me. We got busy guzzling down pints of water, dipping our heads under it and even soaking our helmets. Just what the doctor ordered! The perfect refreshment, at the perfect time, to revitalise us for our final push to Pierre Longue.

Time was becoming a bit of a cause for concern. If we could make it through the next sections and over into the Lindarets valley before the lifts closed we were as good as home. If we got stuck on the Châtel side of the ridge when the lifts closed, we'd have a big climb to get up and over or we'd have a lot of hassle and a long journey to get all the way back round the valleys, over the cols and home.

We cracked on with even more intent than earlier in the day. We made it to Pierre Longue, rode two more lifts and two more liaisons and had got the job done! We were on the

Rochassons lift. The final link to Lindarets and the pressure was off... A bit.

The descent down the bike trail alongside the Chaux Fleurie lift into Lindarets is always great fun and it was a perfect celebration for being back on the home side of the divide. Before long though, involuntary schralping let me know that I'd got another puncture. Thankfully we were near the bottom so I just pushed it the last stretch and got to work while the lads went ahead and stopped at the next food station for snacks and beers this time.

We joined another big queue for the Lindarets chairlift up to Avoriaz. As we waited, we realised we might need to skip the next off-road section at Super Morzine completely and just charge down the road instead. As far as we could tell, the last Pleney lift that would allow us to get back up and over to Les Gets was at 6 pm. By the time we got to the top of the Lindarets lift it was 5.30 pm. We realised we just didn't have time and the road option was the best option. Speed time! We motored down the road from Avoriaz, catching cars up at every switchback and even overtaking a couple. What could have been a bit of a disappointing but necessary detour turned into another high-speed highlight of the day!

We rolled into Morzine, across the suspension bridge, pedalled through town and pulled up at the Pleney lift turnstile with four minutes to spare! Phew!

The last descent into Les Gets from the top of the Pleney was a beauty. We were on the homeward stretch, with the end in sight. We'd all got a second wind and started riding like we were fresh as daisies. The potential to stuff it with the end in sight was significant.

We didn't though. We were fine, thankfully. The deck chairs of the Aprèski Bar were just where we'd left them nearly 10 hours earlier. They beckoned us in as we sped around the last big berms of Roue Libre and skidded to a halt. Hand slaps and fist bumps all round as we peeled-off helmets, packs, pads, and uncomfortable layers and ordered our first round of beers.

After such a long, hot day, covering so many kilometres, those ice-cold beers were like nectar of the gods. We'd been forced to adapt the itinerary but the great company, deck chairs and setting sun topped off a perfect end to an awesome day out!

13 - Camaraderie and Connection

From the outside looking in, mountain biking can come across as a little bit intimidating, especially the descent-focused strains. The full-face helmets, the tinted goggles, the dirt and a penchant for black. The speed, the risk and the potential for harm may all seem a bit menacing.

If you go to a bike park town when the season's in full swing, it can feel like you've stumbled into a minor conflict zone. There are usually a few people milling around with their arms in slings or hobbling about on crutches, waiting for their friends to come back from the front line on the hill. There are even more who've "lost a bit of bark" and are sporting grazed elbows, shoulders or legs like badges of honour.

There's the mix of mud, sweat, exertion, sun exposure, weathering and helmet hair. Combine that with the prioritisation of riding bikes over personal grooming, and it can lead to a somewhat caveman-esque appearance. Add in elevated levels of adrenaline to the recipe and you end up with visions of wild-eyed savagery. Bands of marauding barbarians blasting out of the woods on two-wheeled chariots, grinning, chattering and fist-bumping manically.

Those still on the outside looking in, shouldn't be too quick to judge though... Don't be fooled by those appearances.

From within, and on the whole, this is an awesome tribe. A community of support and mutual respect.

Yeah, there's the odd tool out there, as there always is but on the whole, most people are sound as a pound.

We all love the same thing. We're all sharing a similar experience. We're all on the same conveyor belt of progression from the total noob to the top of the tree. We're all riding the same trails and the same terrain and getting those same awesome sensations.

We're helping each other out, sharing tips and information, transmitting knowledge up and down the chain. Bike handling techniques, trail secrets, line choice, feature tips and speed advice. Where to brake, where to let fly and what to watch out for.

There are those immortal words when an explanation or description is not quite enough, "Do you want to just follow me in mate?" Then, unwavering faith and trust in a comrade take over, to facilitate our next step of progress.

We're passing on technical knowledge, maintenance tips, jokes and stories. And, ultimately, we're looking out for each other if it does go sideways.

We share the highs and we share the lows. We know the feeling of facing the risk and overcoming the fear. We know what it feels like to take a spill. Many of us know what it feels like to be out of action and we know the feeling of appreciation when our mates are there to lift our spirits.

The common experience connects us all and that connection primes the pathway for real-world interactions. The timeframe from meeting a complete stranger to forming a friendship is slashed! "Ah cool, you ride too. Just give me a shout if you fancy heading out for a few laps?" *Boom*! We're off!

In a matter of days, I often find I've ridden with all sorts of people: good mates, new mates, big groups, little groups, on my own, with people I'd only just met, different nationalities, young, old, slow, fast and full-on senders... It's always different and it's always fun.

Our mutual passion leads to the privilege and pleasure of sharing so many peak experiences with our riding buddies. Elevated experiences where we're wired on a natural high, where positive emotions are sky-rocketing and our sense of being alive is through the roof.

We get to share the joy of breaking new ground, celebrating our successes and our personal triumphs. We all know that feeling of popping out of the bottom of a sweet trail, ridden well and screeching to a halt for hand slaps and fist bumps while the whole group is still totally buzzing with excitement.

From the outside looking in, it might seem a bit intimidating but from the inside looking around, this is a community unified by a common passion. It's a big bunch of potential mates, a clan of stoke-seeking souls, united by bike-based fun.

14 - Megavalanche

Just one week after the Passport du Soleil, there was something else in my calendar, something that was causing a significant background fizz of anxiety in my psyche.

I'd been out snowboarding with Jacko earlier that year and he had said, "Hey man, d'you fancy doing Megavalanche this year?"

"Yeah, sounds good..." I said, without really thinking about it. Before I knew it, it was booked and we were going!

Then, before I knew it again, it was almost time! As the dates approached, the nerves started to kick in.

I'd known about Megavalanche for years from the nutty-looking YouTube vids that regularly do the rounds. I'd always thought, *"That looks mental!.. But fun… It's probably not something I'll ever actually do though."*

Well, I was definitely doing it *now*, and neither Jacko nor I really had any idea what was in store.

If you're not familiar with it, Megavalanche is a mass-start, downhill mountain bike marathon race. It's billed as "The longest and craziest DH mountain bike race in the world!"

Hundreds of riders set off at the same time from an altitude of 3300 m at the top of the Pic Blanc, above Alpe d'Huez. They race down the snow of the black Sarenne ski piste before clattering across kilometres of rocky mountain terrain and scree, onto grassy alpine single-track, then finally dropping through miles of dusty, rooty woodland trails; 30 km after setting off, and 2600 m of vertical descent later the finish line beckons. The top boys make it there at around the 40-minute mark!

We'd both been busy in the run-up and weren't able to make it there for the Monday to Thursday practice days. We'd agreed that we'd just travel over on Thursday and hopefully get a bit of practice in before qualification on Friday.

We arrived at lunchtime on Thursday and met up with some of Jacko's mates from the UK who had been there all week practising. They'd done it in previous years and after we'd registered, Jimmer took us up for a practice run on the qualification track and gave us some tips.

He said the qualification track was as gnarly as anything on the main race course so not to worry too much about coming across anything worse than that.

He also said, "Don't let go of your bike if you fall in the snow. It stops but you don't and then you have to hike back up for it."

"The snow gets rutted quickly so get in a rut on the steep bits and get a foot or two down. Back brake on lock and sit on the wheel if that helps."

"On the steep bits, some people jump off the bike and slide on their backs while they hold the bike."

"There's a whole bunch of luck involved in staying clear of crashes, not getting a mechanical problem, and not getting stuck behind slower riders where you can't pass."

As we rode the lift up we also discovered that we were too late to ride the full length of the qualification track. Getting a bit of limited practice on the middle section before showtime the following day would have to do!

Jimmer joined us for the first run, then left us to it for the second. There was barely anyone still riding it but we got chatting to one guy on the lift back up for our second run.

"You've only had *one* practice run!" He said. "What about the main course!"

"We've just got here," we said.

"Oh, OK... Woah," he said, raising his eyebrows and nodding to himself.

Brilliant! Way to crank the nerves up another notch buddy.

Ah well. We'd be fine. There wasn't time to memorise it properly or find the quickest lines but we made a mental note of a few tasty sections to watch out for. Then, halfway down, I got a puncture. Great! If I hadn't been nervous before (which I had been), I was now.

We made it back to town and agreed that getting down in one piece was the main priority and anything else would be a bonus. We got showered, went out to grab a bite to eat, and then hit the sack for a good night's sleep.

I was in the first qualification wave the next morning which meant getting to the DMC lift at 7.30 am. Jacko was a bit later so I got up, got ready and set off on my own for the lift. We had to take the DMC lift to the mid-station before disembarking. There was then a couple of kilometres of pedalling along a track to the Alpette-Rousses lift. Following this, it was on and up to the start point at Le Dôme des Rousses at 2800 m.

It was flipping freezing up there and windy, too. There were probably 100 of us huddled up around the back of a small hut, squished in like penguins. The more people that arrived, the more sheltered it got, which was good. I got chatting to a few guys who once again expressed concerned-surprise that I hadn't ridden the full course. "*Jeeze!*"

As we got closer to our departure time, I had a wander around and a look at the start. I could see we'd be heading down a zig-zagging snowless ski piste, covered in big, sharp chunks of stone.

It's the first time I've competed on a bike, let alone in a mass start. By the time they called us to the start positions and lined us up ready to go, my adrenaline was coursing! They revved us up even more with some techno music, accompanied by a bunch of whooping and hollering! The 30-second countdown came, then 5, 4, 3, 2, 1. HOOOONK! We were off!

The start was frantic as everyone got busy with the pedal strokes. I just sat in with the flow until I realised there was already a huge pile up right in front of me, ahead of the first corner. I managed to swerve around it to the right and fell back in with the pack.

Suddenly, a bloke came flying past me, and the group in front of me, at the next corner. I realised I was going way slower than I was capable of and slower than I needed to be! I sprinted out some pedal strokes, got after him and started climbing places. Just making it down in one piece hadn't lasted long... I was on the hunt!

We'd been told places 1–35 in each qualification heat, would qualify for the main Megavalanche Race; 36–70 would go in the Mega Challengers with qualifiers 71–95 in Mega Amateurs and 96 + in Mega Affinity.

After several switchbacks, a rock plateau, a snowfield and a traverse, the field started to stretch out and we reached the bit we'd ridden the day before. Inexperience and lack of track knowledge were already taking their toll. Riders streamed past on better lines as I followed the masses and skirted for what looked like the "safe" routes.

It was true what everyone said about it being hard to pass and as we descended, we kept bunching up for the more difficult sections. One bloke teetered to a standstill at the top of a small rock ledge only to be knocked off it, sideways by the next guy going into the same place too hot.

Most of us yelled, "Ça va?" and, "are you alright?" but the odd "tool" just got aggy from behind, because of the hold-up. The lad shouted back that he was OK, so we all cracked on.

I was panting like a good'un by now but really buzzing at the whole thing. What a rush! I kept making up a few places, only to lose them again at the technical bottlenecks where a bit more scouting time could have revealed better options.

Two-thirds of the way down there was a little climb on a track and I was gulping air big style. I was looking forward to the next bit though. It was a series of big, high-speed rollers that had been great fun to launch off and crest over on yesterday's practice. Unfortunately, I got stuck behind a bloke who was being a bit more cautious over them than I wanted to be. I finally managed to pass him over the crest of the last one and dived into the next corner.

Twenty-something minutes after setting off, I'd reached the bottom of the DMC lift and the start of the last section before the finish line. This was unfamiliar territory again and I immediately stuffed up by launching off a small blind drop in the cutting for a chairlift station. I instantly discovered that the bank fell away steeply to a flat bed of sharp stone. I landed heavily, bottoming out my suspension and bending my seat with my backside.

Dammit! I'd made all that effort and was going to end up with two flat tyres, this close to the finish line.

I immediately decided that I was just going to ride on whatever state the tyres were in and it was a relief to find that both of them had held up. The extra pressure I'd put in after yesterday's puncture may have made it a bit more challenging on the way down but it had done the trick when I really needed it.

Pedalling into the finish area in the middle of town, I crossed the line. Phew! I was shattered but that was awesome! I was shaking with adrenaline and immediately made friends with a bunch of guys who were in the same wide-eyed, jittery state as me.

I eventually calmed down a bit, snaffled some free cake and drinks and went back up to cheer Jacko and Jimmer on their way down. Stopping at the scene of my seat bending "send to flat", I found I wasn't the only one making that mistake.

A crowd had gathered and there was a collective "Ooooo!" every time a rider launched off it. That was either followed by a collective flagging-down of incoming riders to warn them that someone was un-crumpling themselves from a heap in the bottom, or by a massive "CHEER!" as they landed it and rode out of the other side.

Josh Bryceland came through fast and sent it huge with a fully committed crowd-pleasing "no footer". This was accompanied by a concerned chorus of "Ooooo!" followed by a pause, then a massive cheer as he sped out the other side, unflustered.

Jacko came racing through and I cheered him on before making my way back to the finish line to meet him. He'd got the buzz-jitters too and we excitedly swapped notes as he shovelled in some cake.

At 6 pm we met up at the rider expo village for free beers, trials show and to find our results. Jacko bumped into a bunch of other riders he knew from the Morzine crew and we found out we had done OK. We would be joining Jimmer and some of his mates in the Mega Challengers race the next morning. We'd all be getting up at different times though due to our start line allocations. Jimmer invited us back to their chalet for a huge (and most appreciated!) spread of food before we headed back and hit the sack ready for another early start.

Once again, I was first up and headed out feeling more than a little anxious. This was totally new territory now.

Loading hundreds of people, with bikes, in qualification order onto the Pic Blanc was like a military operation and was extremely well executed by the organisers.

I waited at the DMC for my letter to be called and joined the queue before boarding the lift. We stayed on it past the mid-station this time and got off at the top before joining the next queue (in order) for the Pic Blanc cable car.

Emerging at the top was an interesting sensation. The sky was blue and clear but the air temperature was even colder than the previous morning. It felt like such a small exposed space for the number of us that were already crammed up there. The views were magnificent though, stretching in every direction across the snow-splashed peaks of the surrounding Isère mountains.

Whilst the deck already seemed fully packed with bikes and riders, a constant stream of others were arriving and I knew there were hundreds more to follow. We were directed to stack our bikes in start order and having done that, I figured I'd join the queue for the toilet and get that out of the way in good time.

I queued next to a female firefighter from Essex. We got chatting and the pattern continued when she asked if I'd ridden the course, and when I said I hadn't, she exclaimed "What!.. NONE of it!?"

Just when I needed a bit more anxiety.

She was a seasoned, repeat Megavalancher and caught up with friends every year that she'd made along the way. She reiterated some of the tips Jimmer had given us and talked me through the route. As we queued and chatted I felt myself starting to sway. I was beginning to feel the effects of the altitude and was lightheaded and dizzy. Jeeze! I could do without that as well. Luckily, once I'd had a pee, moved around and got back outside, I felt much better. I wished her luck as she headed off for the start of the women's race.

I had a wander about, to see what was what and watched the e-bikes lining up for their race. I found Jimmer for a quick chat then soon after, Jacko turned up. Before I knew it, they were calling for my qualification group to make our way to the start.

Next thing, I was lined up, squashed in the middle of 200 other guys. We were 3300 m up at the top of a black piste, having had no practice and no real idea of what was to come. I also noticed that my ginormous backpack was not the norm. I'd packed plenty of water, snacks (for some reason?..), spares, tools, first-aid kit, the lot. Haha! I'd definitely be paring that lot down if I did this again. A lot of guys just had an inner tube taped to their frame!

On this occasion, in my case: *Profuse Provision Preparation Potentially Precedes Pants Performance.*

The atmosphere was electric! You could feel it swelling towards a crescendo and ready to break. I squashed my jacket into my pack next to the kitchen sink, swung it back on my back and got ready for the music. The shrill techno beats of 666s Alarma filled the air and every fibre of my being. Then came the countdown, whooping, hollering… "5, 4, 3, 2, 1." HOOONK!!! "*We were off!*"

I didn't make it far down the piste before I lost it and was off and sliding. I'd had a lot of pointers for this snow-covered section but sliding upside down and backwards wasn't one of them. Having tried it, I wouldn't recommend it as an optimal technique. At least I managed to hold on to my bike.

Luckily, a pile-up in front of me gave me a chance to slow down, regroup and give the right way up another go. I started experimenting with no feet, one foot, two feet, knees, sat on the back wheel and eventually settled on seated on the seat with one foot down. I realised my seat was too high though and by the second steep pitch when I eventually binned it, I ended up sliding on my back with most of the bike on top of me which worked pretty well.

The snow was deeper and softer than I'd expected. I guess that's just the luck of the draw. It had started out freshly groomed that morning but it had already had the women and the e-bikes down it before we dropped in. The top group would go first thing tomorrow when it was cold, frozen and freshly prepped all over again.

Jimmer's tips were solid and I passed loads of lads scrabbling back up the slope to retrieve their bikes. They had not kept hold of them and the bike had anchored, and stopped sliding, way sooner than they had.

The field started to thin out and the snowy piste levelled a bit. I'd started getting a good feel for how to best ride the snow when my chain got snagged between the chainset and the frame, leaving my pedals locked in an awkward position. I hung on until I got to the end of the snow and pulled over to un-snag it and hook it back on. Riders flew past panting while I battled to free the chain and get it back on. "Competitive Jim" was back and I was already rueing the fact that I'd wasted good time sprawling around in the snow.

We began to traverse the more rocky section of the mountain, crossing patches of sun-shaded snow on the way. I lucked-out a couple of times by getting in a high rut across these snow banks and overtaking a whole load of people bunched up in a different one. There were a few technical bits here and there where the flow backed up and they were good opportunities to get past if you knew where you were going.

We eventually crossed the ridgeline and started heading back towards the village of Alpe d'Huez. Man! This was full-on! I was pedalling and panting like a madman but feeling the intense buzz of sustained effort and concentration. The track swooped, wound and zigzagged. People were taking spills all over the place.

"Ça va?" and, "You OK?.." Yep! Crack on!

Suddenly my chain jumped off and snagged again, "*Dammit!*" If this thing snapped, I'd be screwed and *well* peeved!

I arrived at a section we'd ridden the day before with the short pedally climb. I'd been gulping air here yesterday but it was even longer today and lined by spectators cheering us on. One of them was in a stereotypical French outfit. He had a stripy jumper and a beret and was dangling a baguette in front of people with a fishing rod to coax them on. "*Haha! Classic.*"

I tried to use the climb as an opportunity to get some water on board but I was struggling to suck it in and swallow between all the puffing and panting.

Note to self: Less water next time would save weight and the eight-course buffet I'd packed was definitely not necessary.

We pedalled up and over another brow and got a glimpse of the village of Allemont in the valley below. It looks like it was still miles below! It felt like we'd been going for yonks and there was still so much left! I was thoroughly enjoying it though.

We'd been down snow, rock, scree, single-track, alpine meadows, an off-road track and were now winding across a hillside and into some seriously dry and dusty woodland. I'd caught up with another group and we were all jostling for position looking to get past people. I got past one, and then my chain snagged. "*For crying out loud!*" It hadn't snapped though so never mind. I got it back on and got after them again.

The woods were great fun and they just went on and on! The dust was making it even more challenging. If you got too close to the people in front you couldn't see the ground, roots, or ruts well enough to properly pick a line. You just had to trust that following the path of the guys in front would work out OK.

The trail popped out onto roads and tracks here and there before dropping back in again. I took the opportunity to pedal hard and sprint past a few people on these wider sections. Others with more beans than me did the same and got past me.

I got some clear air in front of me for a bit, in a section of woodland, so I put the hammer down and started charging. Then, I pushed too hard and hooked a wheel in a corner rut and spat myself down the hill. I didn't lose much time luckily but it was a reminder to just keep it together and not push too hard in these late stages.

Eventually, we emerged alongside a river course and I knew I must be close to the end. A couple more turns and I was in the finish area and across the line! What a freakin' rush! That was awesome! I was in one piece *and* I'd had a reasonably good, clean run.

I guzzled water, ditched my bike and headed off for free food, drink and Red Bull which left me totally wired!

One-by-one Jimmer and his mates came in but there was no sign of Jacko. I gave him a bell to check he was OK. I expected that he would probably be too busy riding to even hear it or answer but he did, and he was fixing a puncture. He'd been making good time but had hit a sharp bit of tarmac edging where the trail popped onto a road and burst his tyre. It wasn't too much longer before he turned up and we joined the hundreds of others excitedly swapping stories in the magnificent July sunshine.

I'd made it down in just over an hour and five which I didn't think was too shabby. I was very pleased with that, especially as there was plenty of room for improvement, although I had been lucky. Jacko was a bit gutted about his flat tyre. He'd been charging through the woods and was going great guns only to hit that snag almost within sight of the finish but still far enough to need to swap it.

Jimmer's competitive time had been compromised as he'd stopped to help someone who'd broken his wrist. It may have scuppered his time but this wasn't his first rodeo and he cemented his status as a class bloke.

The organisers laid on buses to ferry everyone back up to Alpe d'Huez but luckily, another one of Jimmer's mates had driven his van down so we loaded the bikes up and piled on board for the twisty drive back up to town and a well-deserved beer.

All in all Megavalanche was an excellent experience! Well organised, top atmosphere, lots of friendly people and great camaraderie. LOVED IT!

It's definitely addictive though and I think that element of luck causes lots of people to go back time and again. A mechanical issue, a flat, a fall, an injury, or just getting held up, can scupper your qualification chances or your main race run.

I must admit, I spent the following week or so running through all the things I'd do differently to do better. I wouldn't mind going again to spend some time learning the track. I'd love to see if I could actually make it into the main race, make a better job of the snow, find the quicker lines and maybe get down in under an hour... We'll see...

15 - Mind, Body and Soul

Have you heard of grounding?.. There's a theory that reconnecting our bodies with the Earth could have a whole range of positive health benefits. In modern life, we are increasingly insulated from the Earth and direct contact allows us to ground ourselves and balance our body's electrical charge.

Well… Us mountain bikers have been doing that for ages!

Yep… We do it regularly. Sometimes we connect to Earth with our entire bodies. Sometimes we "ground" at high speed, unexpectedly and over an extended distance. Sometimes we even ground face first.

Have you heard of forest bathing?.. The term was coined in Japan in the 1980s but it is simply the practice of immersing yourself in nature. Basking in the forest atmosphere promotes a whole host of perceived health benefits.

Once again!… We've been doing that for yonks!

Yep… We're never happier than when we're in the woods. We'll spend hours, days even, drinking in that woodland atmosphere. We're so enthusiastic, sometimes we'll even hug a tree at 30 km/h.

What about mudding?… Mud baths supposedly increase blood flow and stimulate the immune system, drawing out impurities from the skin and exfoliating. It's even a remedy for sore joints and muscles. A mud bath session in somewhere like New York could set you back hundreds of dollars.

You guessed it… We've been doing that for more than a minute as well!

Yep… You'll regularly find us caked head-to-toe in mud. Sometimes it's even up our noses and on our eyeballs. A rainy day costs nothing and you can be immersed in glorious mud for as many hours as you want. In fact, we regularly mud, ground and forest bathe all at the same time!

Cold therapy?.. Used for thousands of years but it's super popular right now… Every man, woman and their dogs seem to have an ice bath in the garden these days. It's great for muscle recovery, immune system stimulation and all manner of health benefits.

I know… This *is* getting a bit predictable and tedious now but…

Yep… We spend a sizeable chunk of time cold. Often cold *and* wet. Damn cold sometimes due to the amount of time we've been exposed to the low temperatures, damp and wind chill. On many occasions, I've stood in a freezing cold river or stream washing the mud off my bike and myself at the end of a ride. We were doing cold therapy before we even knew what it was.

Connecting to your inner child?... Every damn time we swing a leg over, baby!

When it comes to wellness, we're obviously ahead of the curve but it doesn't end with the pithy parallels. Mountain biking is indeed a veritable feast of goodness for mind, body and soul.

Riding takes fitness, strength, concentration and skill. After a day's hard riding you "feel the burn" in bits of your body and muscles that you didn't even know you had!

Even when it comes to the descents, some people say, "That's not exercise, you're only riding downhill..." Well, I've taken some of those "some" out for a few hours and given it "full beans" until their muscles are pumped and they're panting for breath. It definitely isn't easy if you're riding hard and I don't think I've come across anything else that leaves my entire body feeling so comprehensively "used".

Then there's the mind... Mastering challenging trails, harder features and new skills takes concentration, judgement and persistence. Figuring out manageable steps to maintain progress on a tightrope of self-confidence vs self-preservation with a backdrop of fear management, can be a serious mental workout... Then, there's that point, that moment of commitment, when you've done all the prep and it's time to press "send!"

When it all comes together, the sensations are sensational. Mental chatter dissolves from your mind as your awareness is dominated completely by total focus on the trail ahead. There are times when you're pushing hard and everything melds into a state of "flow".

It's as if you become a passenger to another level of consciousness. Some superhuman part of your mind has taken control, scanning the trail and the obstacles ahead. It zooms in and pans back, running calculations, making adjustments and reacting at speeds that makes your conscious mind think, *"Holy cow! Hat's off big guy. How on Earth are you doing that?!"*

After all that mayhem of speed, noise and physical sensation, as you buzz and grin from a hefty shot from the internal chemical cocktail factory, it's over... You swing your leg back over, load your bike on a lift and settle quietly back into the chair to be peacefully rocked back up the hill like a baby in a cradle.

In my mind, this is the mind/body equivalent of what running out of a hot sauna and diving into an icy lake is for the circulatory system... Sensory assault contrasted with total peace.

Apparently, meditation puts the mind and body in the opposite state to fight or flight allowing it to relax, repair and regenerate. We're going from one to the other and back again in rapid succession.

I'd love to know what scientists could find out about the physiological and psychological effects of that contrast and rotation, but from one practitioner's perspective (me), it feels pretty sweet!

People also say, "The focus and concentration of riding is like meditation". I think it is in a way but in my mind, it's like the total opposite which somehow arrives at the same place. It's as if you set off in opposite directions from a single point on Earth and meet again on the other side.

Meditation commonly involves quieting the input from the physical senses until you experience a deeper awareness that lies beneath. Riding hard on the other hand bombards those physical senses with an avalanche of information and sensation but as you slide into the state of flow you become aware of a greater awareness beyond. Whatever it all is, it's weird and it's cool at the same time.

There's no doubt mountain biking stimulates many aspects of our minds, bodies and souls. There's no doubt that there are rafts of benefits for us physically, mentally and emotionally. In fact, it's almost like mountain biking could be a major factor in maintaining our long-term health in so many more ways than we give it credit for. As if we needed any more excuses to ride.

16 - Oh Bollocks!

When it's going right, it can be some other-worldly, zen-like flow, "*Yeaaah maaaan*" higher state of consciousness shizzle but when it goes wrong… "*FREAKIN' OUCH!*"

If you ride bikes, it's highly likely that you'll come-a-cropper from time to time.

Falling off, crashing, binning it or wiping out comes with the territory, to a certain extent, especially if you're pushing your limits.

I've had my fair share of stacks and my fair share of injuries. Most of us have lost a bit of bark at the very least and know all too well that acid sting as you twist on the shower at the end of the day. Those fine fizzing jets of water make contact with layers of freshly exposed epidermis that were never meant to see the light of day.

I had one particular crash a few years ago which resulted in an injury, a little out of the ordinary. I'm probably guilty of sharing "too much information" on this one but I'm pretty sure people like to hear it, even though it makes them wince.

Maybe I'm a little bit sadistic as well but I'm always amused by watching people's physical reflex reactions when they hear it. They're usually laughing while they're squirming though, so I figure they must be enjoying it on some level, even if it's sheer relief that it wasn't them. If you're a bit squeamish, skip to the next chapter. If not and you're sitting comfortably (maybe with your legs crossed), I'll begin.

When this happened, I'd been living in Les Gets for a couple of years and my riding had come on leaps and bounds. Easy access to so many great trails, regular practice and the influence of some really good riders around me had paid dividends.

I'd got a mate who'd honed his skills in Whistler over several seasons before settling in Les Gets. He was one of those mates that you get on very well with when you bump into them but never really end up spending as much time as you'd like to with them, each time saying, "Yeah, we should do this, or that, or the other" then never really getting around to it.

Well, on this occasion, we did get around to it. We'd bumped into each other and as luck would have it, he was meeting a couple of his mates for a few laps the next day and asked if I fancied it.

"I'm in!" I said.

I had ridden with him before, including on our Pass'Portes du Soleil tour and I knew he was good.

I also knew there were some top-level riders in his circle and it was highly likely that the guys we'd be meeting would be better than me and more experienced. I knew he rode regularly with several World Cup mechanics who are always pretty damn handy on a bike too.

The nervous excitement started to kick in. This was going to be another big boy pants day.

We agreed to meet the following morning at the Chavannes lift in Les Gets. We'd catch the first chairlift and head up and over to the Pleney in Morzine to meet the others.

I got up early, snaffled down some breakfast, got my kit together and checked my bike over. I'd left my homework until the last minute again and failed on the first three of the 7 Ps. The rear brake pads were almost shot. I'd need to pick some new ones up and swap them out on my way to the lifts. That was going to make me a few minutes late, so I fired off a text to Mick, telling him if he needed to crack on, I'd just catch up with him over there later on.

"Nah. No worries. I'll just come and meet you at the shop mate," he said.

I arrived at the shop and asked for new pads. The mechanic fished some out from the stock shelves and said, "Do you want me to put them in for you?"

"Oui, s'il vous plait." ("Yes") I said.

I figured he'd got a stand, and tools to hand and was a professional, so it should save me a few minutes of faffing. Plus, I'd seen Mick pull up, so I could chat to him while the bloke got started swapping the pads.

A couple of minutes later the mechanic ushered me back in the door with an issue. I'm not sure why, but he now had a bleed kit set up on my brakes and was showing me how nasty the brake fluid was. He was telling me that it really needed changing.

"Yeah, OK, whatever." I was conscious that Mick and I had an RDV to make and progress seemed to be going backwards. That nervous excitement that had been building all night was turning into tension.

A few minutes later the mechanic had finished up the bike, I settled up at the till and finally, we were off. We made up time by skipping the lift and link trails and just rolled straight down the main road to Morzine instead.

Mick's first mate met us at the queue for the Pleney lift astride a brand-new Santa Cruz V10 29er. This defo meant business and the fact he was the resort manager for one of the bike holiday operators suggested he was even less likely to be shabby when it came to putting that weapon of a bike to good use. Mick's other mate was running much later than us and would catch up later on.

We boarded the Pleney and headed up for some "Pleney Black" laps. The Pleney Black is a beauty of a track. Fast, long and with a bit of everything to test your mettle. We got straight into it and we got into it fast! Darren obviously fell into the "*Full send*" mountain bike character profile. I brought up the rear and was immediately towed into every bit of the trail faster than I'd ever ridden it before.

Darren was hitting little cut-throughs and freeride options that I didn't even know existed and we were gapping across the track and back into berms all over the place. It was one of those situations where I was in full reactive mode. I was following the line the others were tracing, trusting their experience and judgement for speed and my own ability to relax and react.

We juddered over roots, hooked into ruts, sailed over gaps, railed berms and clattered down rocky bumps all the way to the bottom. We pulled up for big grins and fist bumps when we popped out onto the track at the bottom.

Same again! We did it twice more and with each run I felt more comfortable with the speed and happy tucked in at the back.

At the end of the third lap, Stevie met us at the bottom. I had met him before and as we chatted on the lift up he said he hadn't really ridden this season and was a bit rusty.

As the new kid in this group and assuming that he'd probably be quicker than me, even with the rust, I ushered him ahead of me as we dropped in.

I immediately regretted it as the lead two tore straight away at the speeds we'd spent three runs building up to and Stevie, quite sensibly, was going to give himself time to warm up from a cold start. Unfortunately, I was now tuned in to following the other two at that speed. I was also jittery with adrenaline, excitement and focused engagement.

It wasn't far off the previous pace by any means but my thoughts started to wander.

My mind had stopped being completely consumed with reading the trail ahead, watching the others and doing nano-second calculations to control bodily response. I started thinking about things… I started thinking, *"Damn! Why didn't I just let Stevie bring up the rear until he was warmed up?"* *"I was doing pretty well keeping up with the others."* *"Why didn't I just have a bit more confidence in my riding?"*

We dropped into the woods and started weaving through the corners. My mind continued to beat itself up. I launched off one of the cut-through jumps we'd been hitting on the previous runs that had landed nicely into the entrance to a left-hand berm. This time though, as I moved my weight forward to level out the bike, I somehow clipped the back of the seat and knocked the whole bike forwards and clean out of my hands.

"Oh crap…"

I was now sailing through the air with the bars floating down and away in front of me, my feet separated from the pedals and my legs astride the rear wheel.

I barely had time to register what was going on before my bike nose-dived into the berm and I hurtled down on top of it. I pile-drove my balls onto the rapidly spinning rear wheel with all the momentum and weight of a decent-sized jump coming to an abrupt stop with my balls as the rear brake.

Vvvvrrrraaaaaaaaapppppp(!), went my shorts and my balls. *Munch-munch-yum-yum*, went my back tyre. "Aaah shiiitttt!" Went me.

Stevie pulled up ahead of me and shouted back… "Y'alright mate!?"

"I don't think so," I said. "I think I just wrecked my balls… Let me check."

I pulled the bike off the trail and hunched over to take a look down. There was no need to unbutton my shorts. They and my boxers beneath had been transformed into a mini-skirt and crotchless panty combo.

I gingerly lifted the front of my new mini skirt-style shorts, and gently lifted my old man (which was still there thankfully) to one side to assess the damage… Not good.

I had torn a huge zig-zig rip in my ball-sack. It looked like Zorro had stopped by and given my tatty sack the good news with his sword. The cut was open, juicy and definitely in need of stitches… Quite a few by the looks of it.

Thankfully, nothing had plopped out, nothing was hanging out and it didn't look like I was going to bleed to death any time soon.

As is the way with mountain bikers, the next thing through my mind was a quick mental calculation. It started with an initial self-diagnosis: severity, extent of the injury, treatment, recovery time and ultimately how long it'd be before I could ride again… Soft tissue damage, stitches, a couple of weeks or so maybe? Not too bad.

"Right. Let's get it sorted."

I shouted to Stevie. "Mate. You go on… I've ripped a hole in my nut sack… I'm going to have to go to the medical centre and get some stitches."

"I'll come with you!" he shouted back.

I appreciated the offer but couldn't really see how the company was going to make any difference. There was no point spoiling his morning as well so I said, "Nah mate. You're OK. You catch up with the others. I'll let you know how I get on."

"OK. If you're sure."

I knew if I pushed back up I could join the link trail to Les Gets, get to the medical centre there and be closer to home. I set off up through the woods pushing my bike, waddling like John Wayne and trying to keep my balls from swinging around too much.

When I got to the link trail I rang Nina and said, "Hiya. I've had a crash and ripped my scrotum. I'm going to the medical centre for stitches. Could you meet me there and put my bike in the van?"

I set off riding the trail back to Les Gets, a little more tentatively than normal. Understandably, I didn't bother with the jumps in the mini jump park and opted for the main road for the last section from Gibannaz.

When I pulled up at the medical centre, Nina was already parked in one of the spaces. The sun was shining, the birds were chirping and a junior doctor had settled into an outdoor chair to enjoy his lunch break. He was merrily tucking into his packed lunch and watched passively as I put my bike in the back of the van. I climbed into the back seat and out of sight to let Nina have a look.

She'd been thinking, "*Jeeze! Drama queen. It can't be that bad if he just rode all the way back from Morzine and put his bike in the back of the van like nothing's happened.*"

I sat down and lifted up the gapping flaps of material that were once my shorts and boxers to reveal the carnage beneath. "Oh my God, Jamesie! What the heck!" she said.

That made me laugh and was the first taste of the sadistic pleasure I'd get from sharing this tale.

Nina said she'd wait while I got sorted, so I gingerly climbed out of the van and wandered over towards the door.

"Bonjour." I said to the doctor. "Vous êtes ouvert?" ("Are you open?").

"We are closed for lunch until two-certy," he said, speaking back to me in English but with a thick French accent. "You could go down to Morzine medical centre, unless it is an emergency… What'av you done?"

I lifted the front of my new mini-skirt (the skirt formerly known as shorts) and gave him a flash of the carnage beneath. He immediately stopped chewing, looked down and started packing away his lunch.

"OK… Zat is definitely an emergency," he said. "Let's go now."

"Hey… No… It's alright Dr," I said, "I can wait a few minutes, no problem. Please, finish your lunch first…"

"It's OK," he said, looking up at me with a face two shades pastier than 10 seconds earlier, "I am no longer 'ungry…"

"Oops. Sorry Doc."

He led me into a treatment room. I dropped my pants and hopped up onto a bed and he got to work. He started cleaning the area and inspecting my package which was now retreating and cowering in the corner like a scolded dog. He informed me that the wound looked like the skin had been stretched to its limit and torn (*"No shit Sherlock!"*). He finished cleaning things up and set about stitching me back together.

It was a little awkward and he was much shakier than I'd have preferred so I tried to keep it light-hearted for both our sakes by making some small talk.

As a married, middle-aged father of two with plenty going on, personal grooming was lower on my list of priorities. The fact that my pubes were very similar in colour, gauge and length to his stitch thread was obviously making life quite difficult for him.

I needlessly and embarrassingly apologised for a lack of manscaping and told him how my Gran had always told us to make sure we always had clean underwear on in case we ended up in the hospital. I told him that I had but that I'd never considered grooming would be a useful addition to that rule. This led to an awkward exchange where he didn't have any idea what I was talking about and my attempts to explain seemed to make him even more nervous and uncomfortable. I decided to just shut the heck up and let him concentrate.

When he'd finished up, he said, "That's it, sixteen in total."

"*Jeeze!*" I thought. "*That is quite a few.*"

"The stitches will dissolve on their own so there is no need to come back unless you experience pain, redness, swelling, discomfort or feel unwell. Give it two or three weeks before riding again."

"*A couple of weeks… Not too bad,*" I thought.

Nina was waiting in reception as the doctor and I came out. She said afterwards that he looked even paler and shaken than he had when we'd gone in.

I thanked him and we went on our way.

The lads had stopped for lunch by now and there were messages on my phone asking how I was and wanting photos. They were having lunch after all so it'd be rude not to oblige and help with their appetites. Haha!

On post-crash analysis, I realised that the mechanic had put my seat post up to hang it on the bike stand and hadn't lowered it again. With all the rushing around, I hadn't noticed and this may have contributed to me mysteriously knocking the bike out of my hands in the air.

Who knows? It could just have been rider error, but what I do know is that if I'd had a tighter handle on what was going on in my head, I probably would have noticed it. I realised that I needed to try and avoid letting the tension and anxiety creep in. I've also realised that allowing my mind to wander away from total focus when I'm riding is a common contributing factor to having a "moment". I have to be aware and give myself a mental slap in the face when I notice it starting, to stop it continuing. In fact, I've found that for me, pushing a little harder can help me engage more and concentrate better.

I was back on the bike in just over a week. Three of the stitches didn't dissolve so I snipped and pulled those myself. I'm very pleased to confirm that everything recovered perfectly. All present, correct and fully functioning. Phew!

17 - The Terrain, the Tracks and the Travel

Yeah, it's about the riding, the experiences and the people, but how about a massive round of applause for the canvas on which we get to create and play. Thanks, first and foremost, must go to Mother Nature. Hats off! Awesome job!

Those of us who love mountains, hills and wild places often feel drawn to them by something primal and innate. There's a presence in the mountains, a sense of latent, energetic power. There's a majestic aura that can make us feel completely insignificant, yet totally connected.

Our bikes and our sport allow us to immerse ourselves in the beauty of those mountains and wild spaces. They allow us to interact with the scenery and the terrain. We get to play with the contours, the folds and the fabric of the Earth's crust. We build an intimate knowledge of its surface and textures.

We look at the world through a lens calibrated to find fun lines and places to explore. The contours, the valleys, the streams and the cliffs. The exposed rock, scree-fields and shale. The tracks that pick their way along ridges and the mountain peak descents that might just be worth the effort of an exploratory hike-a-bike sesh.

We soak up the essence and profusion of life that flourishes from the mineral matter. We thread our way through dense woodland, rumble over beds of roots, open up through grassy wildflower meadows and *whomp* through the dampened drifty-ness of fresh loam. We launch off natural hits and touch down on wild transitions. We skid and scrabble down huge slabs of bedrock, compressed into existence over millennia, then heaved and tilted with unimaginable force.

It's easy in this life to be limited by the physical senses though. The things we can see, hear, taste, touch, and smell dominate our attention but we're not just playing with three-dimensional "solid" physical reality here.

We wouldn't be able to do what we do if we weren't frolicking with the greatest invisible, attractive force in the universe… *Gravity!*

We play with gravity as an eagle dances on a thermal or a dolphin surfs a wave. We're utilising its relentless power, constantly making judgements and adjustments to ride in balance. We're using it to extract the most speed, flow and joy from the trails we ride. We're judging where to pump, where to load, where to unload and where to explode! Gravity is as much a part of our canvas as the ground beneath our wheels.

The evolution of the universe has done an excellent job laying the natural, physical foundations for us to enjoy but how about some *MASSIVE LOVE* for all those shapers and trail builders out there who take that groundwork and raise it to the next level!?

These guys take Mother Nature's raw materials and mould them into sumptuous ribbons of pleasure. They sympathetically enhance natural lines or "pimp" them, full-on into elevated states for optimal fun. Those guys are out there in rain and shine, passionately grafting, building, sculpting and maintaining for all our enjoyment.

The best are like the love children of physics professors and artists. A mind-meld of science and creativity. Maybe they were conceived in the broom cupboards of university staff Christmas parties. In fact, maybe it was a Christmas ménage-à-trios miracle with a sports professor. That might explain why most of them can shred like absolute demons on top of everything else!

These guys have the ability to compute complex calculations of mass, acceleration, momentum, resistance and velocity. They transform the solutions into masterpieces of environmentally sensitive, natural construction art. When the equation is a success, the trail works in perfect symbiotic harmony with the gravity engine supplying the juice!

These guys permeate our riding community. They range from anonymous local builders to big-name shapers, leaving their signature stamps on their creative endeavours. Many have evolved into specialist teams and businesses contracted to work their magic for bike parks and competition organisers.

Cheers guys. Your work is much appreciated!

These trails we get to ride are like roller coasters or theme park rides but rather than strapping in and handing over control, we get to take the "reins", to add our own flair and ride how we dare.

Some of these trails are complete works of art. They are stunning sculptures of rock, dirt, and timber. Some take on a life and identity all of their own. Some have become iconic; some have gained near mythical status and some become immortalised as scenes of epic feats of riding bravery and skill.

We all have our preferences and favourites. Our boats are floated by different characteristics and our diverse desires. Some like it technical and natural, some like it fast and flowy, some like it balls-out sendy and some like to teeter on tiny balance beams high in the trees. *"That sure as heck ain't for me! No way Jose! No siree Bob!"*

We've got so many to choose from and so much to explore, for every level and every niche. We've got everything from roller-coaster bike parks to local builds and wild natural trails. There are the famous ones and the hidden gems that we stumble across along the way.

We have the pleasure of getting to know them. We get to learn them and love them, getting faster, flair-ier and lair-ier all the time. We get to revisit old flames, to rekindle old memories and hook up for a few more laps around the block.

Our planet is peppered with these ribbons of rapture and parks of pleasure. There is a whole world of possibility and lifetimes' worth of riding just begging to be explored.

With the exploration comes the travel. We don't just get to enjoy the variety of terrain, trails, dirt, features and builds. With travel, we get to appreciate the countries, the cultures, the climates, the people, the food and the different experiences.

When we travel, we meet local riders from new places, visit local bike shops and mechanics. We meet other travelling riders. We can talk about our common experiences and knowledge from different trails and different locations around the world.

This adds even more dimensions to our camaraderie and more strands to our connection. Once again, we're connected by like-minded desires, shared knowledge and common experiences of the tracks we ride, the terrain we experience and the travel we enjoy along the way.

There's so much to ride, so much to explore and *so* much to enjoy!

18 - Tomowak, Canyon, Roue Libre

I hook the laced face of my Five Ten under the footrest, grab the safety bar with my hand and swing the whole restraint assembly up and over my dipped head, as the chair clanks into the top lift station of the Chavannes Express lift in Les Gets.

There's a new banner telling me to *"Please collect my bike quickly."* I hop off and oblige, fast walking across the grated metal deck towards it. It's standing to attention, hanging vertically on the back of the chair in front.

After several seasons of loyal service, it had been time for the ex-rental Glory to slow down, put its tyres up and enjoy semi-retirement. Full-time service has been taken over by my new Propain Spindrift which I treated myself to at the start of the year. These things have always caught my eye and as a freeride bike bridging the gap between downhill and enduro, I wanted to see if it would do more of what I wanted in a single package. So far so good.

I grab my bar grips with both hands, take a step back and give a little yank to bounce the front wheel out of the yellow bike hook which has lovingly cupped my front wheel as it carried my bike up from the bottom station.

I glance over to the two lifties, leaning on the platform's wooden guard rail and chatting amongst themselves. I give them a nod and a "Merci!"

They haven't done anything for me directly this time but their work in all weathers keeps this whole thing moving and facilitates many hours of good times. They deserve an acknowledgement of appreciation every time in my opinion.

"De rien" ("It's nothing/you're welcome") they call back in unison.

I step up onto my left pedal then swing my right leg over the bike as it starts to roll down the crushed stone ramp and onto the rough ground beyond.

Next descent: Tomowak, Canyon, Roue Libre. This is just a quick one-lap blast for me today. It's a quick fix because I've got other stuff to be getting on with. This'll be a speedy top-to-bottom, no stopping, no messing blat, and a great, high-intensity, adrenaline-fuelled workout.

Tomowak is popular with the vast majority of riders who've ever had the pleasure of riding it. It's a fast, fun, blue-rated, jump fest and it has changed a few times since we've been over here. I wasn't mad-keen on the bottom section changes at first, but I've since learned how I need to ride it and now I love it!

It's easy to complain about a section of trail, but sometimes it just needs a new perspective and a new approach to unlock its treasures.

Tomowak only goes about halfway down the hill back to town. From the "midpoint", there are only a couple of "official" options. The first is to join the red mainline "Roue Libre" and the second involves making a right-hand turn and taking a short roll down the road to another "rider's choice" piste, the black-rated, Canyon.

After Canyon, you rejoin Roue Libre, pass through the mini jump park and on for the final stretch down the four cross track and back to base.

This is a fantastic top-to-bottom combo. First some flowy, jumps and berms. Then some roots, rocks, and free-ride style riding, followed by whichever line floats your boat in the mini jump park and then, the big sweeping berms of the mainline red home. There's pretty much a little bit of everything from blue to red, to black and so much to love.

This little puppy should be on top form today as well. It's another fine bluebird day in Les Gets. There was a bit of rain yesterday which has probably dampened down some dust and left behind a fast grippy line. It's even got the potential to be "hero dirt". That kind of dirt that can drastically elevate your riding and leave you looking and feeling like the dog's bollocks. More grip, more speed, more precision. A few extra dabs on the brakes here and there might be required to avoid any serious over-sends.

I already gave the bike the once over before I left home but *properly connected wheels are always high on my "pre-flight" checks priority list.* I take a quick, habitual glance at the front wheel through bolt just to check it is where it should be and hasn't been knocked loose in transit. I flare my right knee and peep through the gap to check the back one's looking good too.

I'm still standing on the pedals, feathering the brakes, balancing and slowly rolling from the lift ramp. Nobody's dropped into the trails since I got off and there's been plenty of time for anyone ahead to be well on their way so off the brakes and time to drop!

Next stop, Les Gets.

The bike starts to accelerate and I lean it to the right beneath me to steer right and skirt the bank into the top of the trail. A couple of pedal cranks and a gentle pump of two small rollers build a nice bit of momentum. I aim for the little take off to the right that seems to have evolved of its own free will and enjoy some early airtime.

I disappear into the shade of a small bank of fir trees and suck up the roller concealed within. The bike drops into the dip beyond, carrying good speed for the take-off on the right-hand side of the trail.

As you emerge from the trees, this little hit is in full view of the passengers approaching the top of the chairlift. I'm not a massive fan of being watched. It's a bit like someone looking over your shoulder when you're trying to concentrate on something. If I think about it, I can get self-conscious and make mistakes, but on the flip side, there's always a temptation to really send it and look cool. It's a great feeling when it works and you hear a "Yeah buddy!" yelled down from above.

"Sod it! I'm sending it!"

Whoomph! I'm airborne. A little tweak turns the bike flatter in the air and sideways to pick up the hipped contour of the bank to the right and change direction for the landing. I also clear the newly blown-out hole below, which is a bonus.

The ample velocity leads to an involuntary *schralp* at the exit of the berm and too much momentum to even think about the next one. I skip it and style it out, like breaking into a jog when you accidentally trip walking in the street. Hopefully, that whole sequence looked intentional, if anyone was watching from above. Haha!

The mini cattle grid *brrriiinngs* as I cross it and the trail snakes to the right. A magnificent view of Mont Chéry fills the vista. A badass-looking Roc d'Enfer hovers menacingly behind Chéry's shoulders like a hulking, granite, close-protection security team.

The trail swings left and forks into two: left for Coaching Track, right for Tomowak.

"Stay off the brakes, hold that speed Jimbo and away we go!"

Crruuuuffff! Rail the big left-hander berm and a big pull to clear the first table. *Crrruuufff,* lock into the right-hander berm.

The banked roller whirls into view. I aim for the centre and give it a little preload and pop just to crest it for the sensation. A nice table follows *whoomph!* I love how this section of the trail builds. Each bit pulls you in to go faster and bigger.

Absorb the landing and eyes ahead for the next longer table, "Y*eat!*" Pleasant airtime and another *whoomph* on the landing. *Badadan-badadan-badadan-dan* over a series of breaking bumps and point that front wheel toward the little kicker on the right-hand side of the trail.

It's set up to jump riders into the left-hander berm but it needs a little respect because it's a "pinger".

It's one of those little jump take-offs that can compress your arms more than expected and fire your back wheel up while you're caught unawares. Like a rodeo… But it's not my first rodeo… I'm ready for it… We're already acquainted. "*Don't be a passenger Jim lad.*" Relax, then attack at the right moment and… "*Use the ping Luke.*"

Ping!.. Float… Touchdown, and slot in to rail the left-hand berm at full bore. "*Wahoo!*"

Stay off the breaks and feel the sensation of weightlessness up and over a big hump. Into the big trough beyond and then a steep, double step-up-ish-thing.

This is actually one of my favourite jumps in the whole of Les Gets Bike Park. It's not massive or full-speed. It hasn't been sponsored with a sign and isn't in full view of spectators but it just seems to give you such a perfectly balanced lift-off and inordinate amount of airtime. It delivers such a beautiful, weightless and floaty sensation. I've thrown some of my biggest and most stylish (in my own head anyway) whips on this little beauty and "*Here we go!.. Oh yes! That's the sugar!*"

There's no time to bask in post-aerial bliss. A big right-hand berm needs my attention. I need to stay off the brakes and hold my speed for the next table and a decent huck to clear the second. "*Yeah boi!*"

I pump the suspension and pop for maximum air off the next little roller to hip onto the bank on the right-hand side. Then it's full speed into a clearing in the trees and past the big log gateway of the Indians' kids' ski piste in the winter.

This is a natural pause point and a group of lads have pulled up on the right for a chinwag. No pausing today for me and I keep my speed up and feel the eyes inspecting my bike as I whizz past and tuck in, beneath the grassy lip of the next left-hander. Float over the small rise, vision right and rail the rollercoaster right-hander, ready for a nice straight section of multiple airtime.

This is another section that pumps and builds to a crescendo. A small table first, "*Woo! Yeah boi!*"

Once upon a time, I passed a guy in a nasty pile here, preparing to be stretchered off. That always flashes into my head for a nano-second on the way past and I always shove it out again ASAP.

On the next feature, I was in a pile of my own at the start of the season. I could get up and ride on thankfully but it was painful, for a long time. This feature is a kind of step-up step-down, on-off thing. Not a big feature and nothing to it by any means.

The sun had been low that day though and the shadows from the trees helped me misjudge the tiny lip take-off for the step-up. It may be tiny but I was trucking-on and the misjudgement meant that I popped for the jump the same split-second that my front wheel dived into the dip behind it and it all went horribly wrong… I hurt myself but it was also one of my first outings on the new bike and smashing it on the floor like that caused me quite a bit of mental pain too. Sorry bike.

No shadows and no problem this time though. Pop onto the top and huck off, back down, out of the trees and into the open.

Fun times ahead now with two, tasty tables. Each one with an extra, larger, launcher ramp built in. The first is to the right and sweeps up and to the left. The next table has the opposite with the larger launcher starting on the left and sweeping up and to the right.

"*Keep the speed Jamesie*"… *Scruuuumph!*… Silence… *Scruuumph!..* Silence… *Scruuumph!..* Two tables and a whip each way… Well. A whip one way (my favoured direction) followed by an awkward-looking effort in the other.

My speed is building through this section. It's being boosted each time as I defy gravity with each lift-off, then embrace its support pumping into each landing transition. Building momentum like a kid on a swing, repeatedly fighting and embracing gravitational pull. A rhythmic alternating pattern. The snarl of the tyres on dirt, then the silence of flight, snarl, silence, snarl, silence.

There's a soundtrack and a rhythm to riding bikes and to sections of trail. You can tell how well you're riding a familiar trail just by the audio feedback and vibrations alone.

Two doubles follow the tables. The second is bigger and I transition left to right as I sail over the dip and set up wide to the right for the entrance of the left-hand switchback berm.

A change of flow for the next two tables feels like fun. I lean back slightly and squash the jump of the first, extending my legs to maintain ground contact with my rear tyre and manual across its length. I shift forward, bend my knees, scoop up the rear and pre-hop into the landing.

I shift my weight forward on the take-off of the second, straighten my arms and push the front wheel down to make contact, while the rear wheel stays airborne. I let the front tyre roll across the surface of the table for a moment, then I pick it back up, throw my weight rearwards and extend my legs, pushing the rear end of the bike forwards in front of my hips.

This is a work in progress. I'm trying to get my weight back far enough to land the transition on the rear wheel and manual away. It still needs work, but it looks damn cool when it works and I'm getting there.

My vision tracks ahead round the corner to the right and I slot the front wheel into the start of the berm. Off the brakes, pump into the apex, launch and open 'er up for the exit. Maximum exit speed for the next section.

Now then, this is the bit I didn't like when it was changed but I've got it dialled now and I love it.

A little double first – pump it.

Then a triple… Three humps… The middle's the biggest, followed by the first and then the last. Squash the first, launch the second and pump the landing on the third. A lovely audio soundtrack through that bit now, confirming maximum speed for the next jump.

This jump was a table that identified as a hip and has ended up as a bit of an angled, leaning table. I stay right which sends me higher and further and plops me right onto the landing sweet spot.

"Breaking bumps incoming!" I stay high and to the left for a smooth ride and prepare for two more bigger tables. Fade to the right and skim the bank on the first one, 'cos it feels sexy, then send the second which always needs a big huck just to make sure. There are no consequences to coming up short but clearing it well is always a personal mini-challenge.

The next two berms are prone to holes and blowouts. Left first, then right. Eyes peeled, picking the fastest line whilst avoiding the biggest divots and corresponding compressions.

One more "yeat" over the last table with a disconcerting tree on the right of the landing, then a straight roll and bit of a breather.

"Roue Libre" joins from the right here so I take a quick "lifesaver" glance to check all's clear at the merge point. Then it's time for three of the finest, perkiest little berms in all the land and that's all she wrote!

The end of Tomowak. A pleasure once again.

It's not over though. I'm on a top to bottom, non-stop mission. Straight ahead is Roue Libre, just to the left of the winter-season-beginners-conveyor-belt-ski-lift. That's a bit of a mouthful which is why "Magic Carpet" is a much more popular name.

I turn immediately right instead and set off rolling down the 4x4 track towards the collection of chalets and restaurant buildings at the top of the Chavannes Télécabine bubble lift. Another mouthful which is why "Red Egg" is a much more popular name.

From the track, I ride onto the road and roll down it towards the entrance of Canyon. It's a pleasant contrast to be back on tarmac for a moment and it's a great opportunity for some manual practice before the mayhem begins.

The bank of public bins next to Canyon's entrance draw in and I glance down the road to check for oncoming traffic, then behind for approaching. "*All clear!*"

I swing out across the road then swoop back left and give it a little pop off the edge of the tarmac and launch into the first section of Canyon.

It's more logging road than bike trail for the first 20 m, as I chatter over the churned-up surface, but after that, the real business begins. The track arcs left and disappears into tall undergrowth and straight into a channel of exposed roots. *Bap, bap, ba-ba-ba-bap!* "*Don't make eye contact with the big tree stump on the right, Jim lad.*"

The shoulder-high undergrowth lining the trail opens into a wooded glade with a web of roots. Stay left of the small trees on the right and spot the big one on the left. I mentally chart a direct course just to the right of it and dance over the top of the roots. "*Nice and loose.*" Placing the bike on my optimal line but letting it move around without going too rigid or resisting.

Over the crest, spot the berm at the bottom, off the brakes for the incline and *Ba-ba-bap!* "*Dropping!*"

Bum out left, elbow high, eyes right and *scrunch(!)* into the left and a nice little pingy jump. The take off conceals the deluge of complex mental calculations looming beyond and the first taste of why this run's called Canyon.

The trail funnels into a narrow trench with high banks on either side. The base is lined with tree roots and rocks, steps and the odd tree stump. Trees and tall stumps rear high on the tops of the banks on either side, dashing by at head height.

I've got preferred lines through here but sometimes I come in too hot, miss my line early on and have to hand over to old-faithful, subconscious autopilot. It usually senses the panic and dutifully jumps into the driver's seat.

This time, it's all good though. Manual controls are sufficient. I bobble over the roots, down the steps, thread to the right of a big stump, hold the speed and I swerve right, up and out of the channel between two "gatekeeper" stumps. I unweight the tyres over a small bed of roots as I keep tracking right to hit the first of two gap jumps in the woodland glade.

The first jump always looks big, because it appears fast and you can see there's a tree stump to clear in the gap but it's no biggy and is always a very pleasant jump. I sail over it and watch the stump pass below.

If the first goes well, the second is a piece of cake and it's just more of the same. The third, I always skip. It's a banked take off. You take off cornering to the right and land cornering to the left. I skip the take off and hop straight into the left-hand berm ready for a short section of flat corners.

I keep my weight low and on the outside of the bike to hold grip through the flat dusty corners. All the while, I make small adjustments to avoid the semi-exposed, smooth snaking roots.

Some of these dirty little beggars follow the trail lengthways but at a slight diagonal. They have the potential to subvert your front wheel on a wet day and dump you unceremoniously in a heap. "*Not today suckers!*"

The section culminates in a small drop, off a cut tree stump and a couple more insurgent roots but I'm all good and ready for some more proper canyon-style action!

It's deeper, darker, rockier and narrower here. A series of steps keep the engagement level high as the trail weaves down the gully. Rooty banks whir past at head height. I do my best to stay loose. Arms and legs, soft and open, allowing the bike to squirm around, independently slotting itself into a nice line along the bottom of the channel. I try to stay balanced and relaxed, keeping my body insulated from the real chatter and only intervening to redirect, adjust, pop and compress where necessary.

The proximity of the banked walls and the meandering intensify to a climax before gradually receding as the canyon sides fold back out into open woodland.

Two newish, man-made, "gap" jump additions are approaching. These have added a little "Je ne sais quoi" to an otherwise chilled bit of the trail. The first one is simple enough and I point, shoot, send and enjoy. The second needs a bit more technical attention (for me at least). The sweet spot on the landing transition is slightly left of the take off. For me, the ideal approach is compromised by a couple of trees and some disconcerting roots.

I favour landing the first jump and skirting to the right of the trees then hitting the second take off from that direction, and that's exactly what I do *"Yeat! Yeah buddy!"*

Better/braver/younger riders than me take the direct route over the awkward-looking roots between the trees. It's definitely quicker and whilst I've only ever seen success, I'm sure there's potential for an arse-twitcher or an unexpected pile driver.

I touch down and crack on. The ground is still more "flat plains" and less "canyon" here as the trail meanders through the trees. The roots have dried and I roll at speed, bopping and bobbling over them without too much concern.

I *do* have some mental notes of a few stumps, rocks and pronounced roots in this section. Some of the roots look like they're making a break for it and chasing their dream of becoming a new tree. These little shysters have caught me out on more than one occasion. Following these silent assassins, there's a rickety wooden "bridge", an awkward little root-riddled lump, a few mild corners and then it's back into canyon territory time.

"*Wahoo!*"

This is a good bit… Everything feels so much faster and more intense when the banks are up high and whizzing by at head height. There are fewer steps in this section. It's strewn with loose rocks as it progresses but there is an obvious, smoother line and you can let it go more and more as you get into it. "*Let 'er rip Jimbo! Wahoo!*"

A quick handful of brakes before the big catch berm at the bottom. It sucks in the suspension then pings me, almost at a right angle to the left, to merge with the link trail back to Les Gets from Morzine.

If I'm riding with mates, this is often the scene of one of those barbarian-esque, wide-eyed, manic-grinning, burst out of the woods and pause for fist bumps scenarios. I'm solo today though and on a top-to-bottom race-run style mission, so instead, I pedal like buggery along the single-track cutting across the ski piste. I cross a small wooden bridge and then merge cautiously onto Roue Libre snaking in from the left.

I'm high and early in the big right-hand berm, avoiding some rocks that have taken the wind out of my sails, and tyres in the past. Getting in high and early makes for a good line to get into the next left-hander nice and early too. Then, I can get off the brakes for maximum speed through the apex, exit, down, up and across, to the top of the mini jump park.

A few years ago there was an option to bank straight into the mini jump park from here, and I liked that. You could keep your flow and keep moving. Now everyone is funnelled to the drop-in area of the mini jump park. Even if you don't have to wait, you still have to almost come to a standstill and double back on yourself to drop in.

I know this is probably a safety measure at a bottleneck like this, implemented with good reason by someone who knows better than me so I'll just shut the fffffff...ront door and quit complaining.

There's no queue this time though and the middle line loses the least speed on the hairpin corner. Actually, the left line does but it's not as much fun, so middle it is. Four tasty tables are lined up and beautifully constructed to build my speed, amplitude and glee on each one. Manual the first, nose bonk the second (getting better), whip the third and bar hump the fourth. *"Yeah buddy!"*

Stick the landing *whooph*, clatter into the traffic calming berms at the bottom, right, left, right and away down the stoney track. I always enjoy a bit of manual practice down here, alongside the pump track and before the final section of Roue Libre.

They call this last section the "four-cross" track. I've not seen it used for four-cross racing in my time here but it's big, wide, fast and bermy. Most of it is visible from the base area at the Front de Neige and L'Aprèski Bar. You can watch a near-constant stream of riders winding and jumping their way down all summer long like some giant, continuous, Donkey Kong-style platform game.

I peel off the stoney track and in between the bank of trees for two on-off jumps back-to-back.

The vast majority of riders in Les Gets end up funnelling down and riding this bit of trail and as a result, some of the braking bumps can be brutal. I give it a big pull off the step-down of the final on-off and send it deep into the landing, carrying maximum speed into the first left-hand battered bump-ridden berm. *Brrrraaaaaaappppp* through the braking bumps. *"Oh yeah! That's a workout."*

Rail the next berm round to the right, step down, rail the big berm to the left, tabletop, right-hand berm, step down… Just when it seems like it's getting a bit predictable there's an option to ride on top of the next left-hander berm and to hit a little jump to drop back into the exit.

I take it and it sets up nicely for a gap jump into the next right-hander, *"Yeah buddy!"* Now stay off those brakes for the biggest yeat of this whole section and I send it as hard as possible right in front of the big, blue LES GETS sign. *"Wahoo!"*

Scruunch into the landing, rail the left and drop down to the next right-hander which is timbered out. One more left-hander and full chat to the finish. Done and dusted!

"Ahh. That feels good!" A nice little fix of exercise and excitement. My heart's racing, lungs are pumping, my body is tight, hard and engaged. Big smile is installed and feel-good chemicals are lapping around my system in abundance. Life is good.

That should keep *"Doo it, doo it"* at bay for a little while.

19 - Freeride

Freeride! What a word. One of my favourites in the English language and made up of two of my other favourites, "free" and "ride".

How many good connotations does free have when you apply it to things?.. Free time, free gift, free-bies. Creatively free, physically free, financially free, mentally emotionally or spiritually free.

Same goes for ride… You can ride loads of fun things: bikes, boards, roller-coasters, horses, water slides and even other humans! There are also plenty of things that can take you on a ride like movies, stories, journeys and adventures.

Actually, I just checked and it looks like "freeride" isn't quite universally accepted as part of the English language.

Dictionary.com says, *"No results for freeride."*

"Whaaaat! You been livin' under a freakin' rock bruv?"

The Oxford English Dictionary online insists on hyphenating *"free-ride"*… That makes it feel more like free-loading to me and that's *definitely* not it.

Collins dictionary comes to the rescue though, defining freeride as, *"A style of skiing, snowboarding, or mountain biking with no set rules."*

"Yeah boi! That's a bit more like it."

That's definitely more like it and that's where it started but I think it can be applied to more sports and more activities in life than just those. In fact, I'd probably define my entire approach to life as a little bit freeride.

Freeride for us mountain bikers is basically anything that isn't in a race format and is more than a plain old cross-country pedal. It covers everything from riding local trails, and squirming through loamy woods, to hitting jumps, big drops, gaps and features (both natural and man-made). It even covers heading out on a major hike-a-bike for more elevation and to get even further from the beaten path.

Dirt jump, park, slopestyle and big mountain riding have all slipped into the freeride pigeonhole, but I still reckon the vast majority of mountain biking could probably be slotted in there alongside them.

Freeride is perfect for today's world of digital content and social media where riders' creativity and skills can be recorded, shared and rewarded within the community and beyond.

As always, there's a sharp end. There's a cutting edge where people are coalescing to push and progress the sport. They are advancing and creating for our entertainment and viewing pleasure. Sometimes I'm not even sure "pleasure" is the right word actually. Watching some of these things can be like eating super-sour sweets or seriously spicy food. There's a pleasure/pain element. You watch with your heart in your mouth as riders lay it all on the line and push the boundaries and limits to breaking point. It's fun, but it's uncomfortable.

A freeride event I stumbled across relatively recently and one which makes for some insanely butt-clenching viewing is the "Tour De Gnar" in Squamish BC.

This event is still in its infancy relatively speaking and has a more traditional/natural freeride lean than many of its counterparts. Riders throwing down on the basalt and granite buttresses in the temperate rainforest of British Columbia. In the latest 2023 edition, Yoann Barelli took 30 riders on a tour of 15 ridiculous freeride features in a single 15-hour session. High stakes, massive consequences, superhuman skill, precision judgement and humongous cajones (and ovarijones)!

Another freeride event that I've already mentioned is the Crankworx Slopestyle event. This approach to freeride uses features that are fully man-made on which riders compete, displaying their creativity, style, skill and technical ability.

The Fest Series is another event format that has proved to be hugely popular. Not content with the confines of existing freeride events at the time, (and in true freeride fashion) a group of the world's top freeriders broke away and did something completely new. They started building high-speed tracks with the biggest jumps ever ridden on mountain bikes. Of course, within minutes of the first successful landing, the tricks began. The popularity of the "jam" format at the first couple of venues has blossomed into a high-speed, super-sized series that spans the globe.

Perhaps the apex event for the freeride mountain bike world is the utterly bonkers Red Bull Rampage. It blends a little bit of all of the above and has reached far beyond the mountain bike community, seeping into the consciousness of the general population.

Rampage is an invitational event held in Zion National Park, Virgin, Utah every year where riders compete for points and the win. They are given a week, hand tools and a limited number of sandbags with which to pimp Mother Nature into a giant freeride/slopestyle course.

The competition canvas always reminds me of a drip sandcastle of Goliath proportions. Riders drop in from a high peak in the Martian-esque landscape. They compete for points, being judged on criteria such as difficulty of line, technical ability, complexity, control, fluidity, tricks and style.

There are insanely exposed ridge lines, near vertical chutes, 20 m canyon gaps, 20 m drops and more to navigate before reaching the finish line on the plain below. If that's not nuts enough, riders are throwing down front flips, back flips, supermen, suicide no-handers, tail whips and anything they can come up with to impress as many points as possible out of the judges.

The results are a breathtaking spectacle of creativity, courage and skill but I'm not sure how many more I'll be able to watch live. It's intense! It definitely produces a spike in cortisol levels, blood pressure and heart rate.

Having said that, I like sour sweets and seriously spicy food. The memory of any adverse effects from those always seems to wear off over time so I guess I'll keep watching for now. Actually, I would love to go and watch it in the flesh sometime, to really soak up the spectacle and the atmosphere.

These four events highlight the nature of freeride at the cutting edge, but other than describing the style of riding like this, there *is* another use of the word freeride in our mountain bike circles which doesn't seem to pop up on the radar of the language aficionados.

We MTBers don't just use it to describe the style of riding but we also use it to describe some of the trails themselves. The "unofficial trails", the "secret trails" or (*raises fingers for the inverted commas*) the "*'locals' trails*"… The "freerides".

For Love of Mountain Biking, Dictionary Suggestion ;)

Freeride

noun

1. Undertaking an activity (particularly skiing, snowboarding or mountain biking) in a free and creative manner without set rules or the need to conform to precedent.

2. A mountain bike trail or line which is not part of a designated bike park or trail centre trail.

\-

These "freerides" are akin to an off-piste run in snowsport terms. It wasn't actually part of my vocabulary like this until I moved out to France, where I discovered French and English riders alike using the term to describe the non-bike park trails.

These trails are usually more natural and less manicured than their managed counterparts. Most have appeared gradually from the footfall of animals, people and/or the passage of bikes. Some have had a little help with a catch berm here, a kicker there or a bridge somewhere else. Sometimes the "tree fairy" comes out after winter and clears the new fallen ones that are blocking the path.

These freerides can range from a tight string of single-track through the woods to a series of huge or lengthy man-made features, hidden in the back of beyond.

They also regularly come with an R-rated moniker which can make life a little awkward. I've had a few toe-curling moments when I bumped into French riding buddies when my kids were younger.

The Frenchies were oblivious to the language implications and proceeded to tell me how they'd just been riding "Your Mum" and then had a couple of laps on "Donkey D***" before finishing on "Buffalo F*****".

"Errrr... Just close your ears for a moment will you kids."
"Yikes. Haha!"

I should perhaps mention that oftentimes, these freerides exist in peace but sometimes they can be a bone of contention, especially if they cross someone else's property without permission. They can be a major cause of friction and the legal and liable implications for the landowner will obviously vary across the world from location to location.

In an area like this, it's a tough one. The cat's out of the bag to a certain extent. There are so many riders in the same area and more visiting for more of the year. I don't know what the answer is but I'm certain that as riders, we'll get furthest if we act with as much respect, consideration and appreciation as possible.

Anyway... Whatever.

I rest my case… Whether we're talking about the disciplines, the trails, the word or the connotations, it's hard to argue that "freeride" isn't the absolute nuts!

20 - Châtel River Gap

The Châtel River Gap is what it says on the tin. It's a big ol' gap across a river in Châtel. It's probably more of a stream technically but let's not beat about the bush, it's a decent size gap requiring respect and commitment.

Astonishingly, it can be found on the blue trail called People, where it forms a little detour. It is by no means a blue feature though and the warning signs on the trail should be well heeded.

It's also cool because you get a great view of it from the Pierre Longue chairlift. I often take non-riding "civilian" visitors on a chairlift tour in the summer. You can ride up the Chaux Fleurie chairlift from Lindarets and down the Rochassons, then Pierre Longue chairlifts to the base at Châtel Bike Park and then ride them all the way back again. If you're lucky, you'll catch a few riders racing through and sending it over the river gap.

Now, the first time I saw someone hit it, I thought *"Holy Cow! Sod that!"*

I know there are way bigger features out there but this one does look impressive for something so accessible. It's got some character, exposure and some infamy.

I've heard many stories since that first visit and met people who've got it wrong or know someone else who did. In fact almost everyone's got a story, from people ending up in the river bed with broken femurs to people coming up short and splattering themselves or getting bucked on the landing and pinging a collar bone.

The name, the visibility and the stories, all add to the magnitude and the menace. The shapers have added in some catch-netting and a crash pad which is nice, but they don't look like they'd help a great deal if you did get it wrong and possibly make it look even scarier.

That first summer in the PDS, I'd ridden in Châtel quite a few times, mostly with Jacko. Châtel always has a "next level" feel when you ride over there. Everything just feels a bit more extreme and a bit gnarlier. Sometimes the greens don't always really feel like entry-level trails. In fact, I've taken novices over then turned round after one run and gone somewhere else. There's even a "Vink" line, built by the man himself which kind of sums it up. I'm not complaining mind you. It's flipping cool.

On one trip, we'd driven over to Lindarets before getting the chairlift up and over to access Châtel. We blasted down the ever-fabulous Panoramique which snakes along the Lindarets side of the ridge before crossing the lip, doubling back and snaking along and down the Châtel side of the ridge. This is a fabulous ribbon of a green trail. It's beautifully constructed so that everyone from novice to expert gets big thrills from riding it.

We hooned around the place for a while, hitting the usual suspects and scrabbling down a couple of blacks for good measure. As we rode up over the river gap on the chairlift,

Jacko looked at me and said, "Hey man, would you mind getting a photo of me doing the river gap?"

"Yeah, sure," I said, "No problem."

He'd done it before but from that point on, his demeanour completely changed. It was like I was with a different person. He went quiet and pensive. He stopped chatting and it felt like he'd gone all serious, which he had! I read the room and kept my mouth shut. I just let whatever was going on in his head play itself out.

We rode the rest of the lift back up in silence. Then, we rode down the first section of trail before popping out at the natural "pause-point" in the ski piste clearing. The access to the section with the river gap was just ahead of us.

Jacko licked his lips, shifted nervously and said, "Give me a ring on the phone when you're in position and ready. I won't answer but I'll set off."

"No probs, mate," I said, pedalling off to get in position and feeling pretty nervous for him. I started running through all the scenarios of what I'd need to do if it didn't go well, "*Block the trail from above with my bike; check how he was; first aid if necessary; pray that mouth-to-mouth wouldn't be necessary; call emergency services on 112; location: River Gap on People, Châtel Bike Park.*"

I got in position, down the trail, to the right of the landing and looking back up at a diagonal. It should make a nice pic from there. I flicked off my gloves, pulled out my phone and unwrapped it from its repurposed protective sock. I scrolled down through to "recents", found Jacko and pressed the call button. I lifted the phone to my ear, heard it connect, ring once and then cut out.

"*Hmmm,*" I thought... "*I wonder if he got that?*"

I stood there for quite a while with the phone camera pointed at the jump, just in case, but there was no sign of him. "*It mustn't have connected at his end.*"

I lowered the phone and clicked the home button to give him another ring. The instant I tapped the button, he came hurtling around the corner, launched the jump, sailed through the air, cleared the gap and landed perfectly. "Did you get it?" he shouted as he sped past.

"*Oops…*"

He didn't fancy another take.

He assured me it was no big deal and that he was just pleased to have done it again. He'd returned to his normal self as well thankfully. He was back out of concentration mode, excited, satisfied and free to just enjoy riding again for the sake of it. "Don't worry, we'll get a pic next time, mate," he said.

It didn't take long. We went back a couple of weeks later and he went quiet again for half an hour before launch. We refined our protocols and agreed that *actually speaking on the phone* once I was in position was probably a better move than the letting-it-ring fiasco. He sent it again and I got a great pic. I remember thinking, "*There's no way I'll be doing that.*"

A couple of seasons later, we'd agreed to meet up for a day riding in Châtel. We were well into the season and it'd be the first time we'd made it over there that year.

Commitments had increased in the two years since that first summer of freedom. My free time had become more scarce as our lives had settled into more of a "normal" existence. Commitments and responsibilities may have increased but so had my riding ability and confidence.

We rode out from Les Gets this time, up the Chavannes and down over to Morzine. We rode through town, up the Super Morzine and Zore lifts before a couple of laps on the runs into Lindarets. Here, we jumped on the Chaux Fleurie lift and then blasted down our old mate Panoramique.

Jacko had already started jabbering on about the river gap as soon as we set off. Now, he was saying that he wanted to get it done sooner rather than later so he could get it out of his system and forget about it.

We rode People to scope out the run-in for any changes, then saw a couple of lads send it as we rode the chairlift back up and over.

He broke from his quiet preparation mode to say, "See mate, it's easy."

We descended the top section of People again and pulled into the natural pause point in the clearing of the ski piste and drew to a halt.

"Are you going to do it then?" he asked. ("*Man! It's making my heart pound just thinking about it again as I write this.*")

"I don't know," I said, "Maybe I'll follow you in and if I clear the squirrel catcher (filter feature – a jump in this case), I'll know I've got good speed and I might go for it…"

I'd stuck my GoPro on my chest mount for the day to catch some footage. That meant "camera courage" was in play. Camera courage can be both a good thing or a bad thing. Good because it helps with commitment which is important but bad because it can make you commit to something that's beyond your abilities, although, either way, you're likely to get some good footage.

I took some deep breaths, checked the GoPro was recording and we dropped in. Jacko led the way… We built good speed through the trees and the corners, over the little stream gap and into the table-tops. By the time we reached the last tabletop, we were flying! I touched down perfectly on the transition of the last table and was lined up beautifully for the gap.

Split-second decision. *"Screw it, let's do it!"*… The kicker was upon me in an instant and *"Shhhiiii!"* Take off! *"Ooff! That feels high"* and … Touch down!.. *"I made it!.. Yes!"*

We were still absolutely motoring when we landed and it was about five more corners before I'd managed to gather myself enough for an audible "Wahoo!"

"Did you do it?" Jacko called back.

"Yeah man! WAHOO!"

For the next 20 minutes I was *totally* fizzing with adrenaline!

I'd steadily progressed to the point where I'd done something that I'd never dreamt I'd do. I hadn't even set out to do it that day! It was a bit of a revelatory moment actually. It had reminded me that there was really no need to place expectations or limitations on anything... Never say never.

The whole Châtel River Gap journey had been a perfect example of that wonderful MTB progression thing again. An awesome, addictive and rewarding aspect of our sport. We find a new challenge, fear it, look at it, suss it out, talk to people about it, practice elements of it, improve our riding until we're confident we can do it, trusting our judgement that we're ready to go and finally letting it all go and going for it! And when it works out, it feels amazing!.. Maybe *I'll* get a pic of me doing it one day.

21 - Resilience and Resourcefulness

Resilience, resourcefulness and self-sufficiency are seen as high-value attributes in modern life. They are key skills we are supposed to be instilling in younger generations, both for their own well-being and for the benefit of wider society.

Mountain biking requires these skills in abundance and it builds them almost as a byproduct. We don't even notice that we're increasing our reserves and developing these skills because we're busy having fun. We're just focusing on pursuing something that brings us buckets of joy.

Resilience, grit or determination is reinforced by pushing through adversity and keeping going. The more we do it the stronger we get. Sometimes we've got to dig deep to get up a climb or keep pushing when it'd be easy to stop for a rest or throw in the towel.

Sometimes we've just got to crack on when it's cold, wet and miserable. We might even have to force ourselves to get up and out there when we can't be bothered or it looks a bit minging. We always know we'll be rewarded though. We know it'll be worth it once we're out there smashing it and having fun.

We push and persevere to master new features, skills, tricks and tracks. We continue through trial and error. We keep progressing despite the setbacks or mishaps because we know we'll get there. The process *and* the result, are worth the effort. Every time we push, we're building that resilience and grit.

We practice taking control of our own minds. We become aware of our thoughts and our automatic responses. We have to objectively assess the fears and the doubts, and when the time is right, we have to overrule the uncertainty. We have to assert our mental dominance, quiet the mental chatter, take charge and say, *"OK, enough! Pipe down… We've got this. It's time to commit."*

It's not uncommon to have to deal with an accident once in a while, whether it's a mate or even a stranger. This can throw us suddenly and unexpectedly out of our comfort zones, calling on new depths and reserves of resilience and resourcefulness. Experiencing these states and situations makes them more familiar and if we ever find ourselves in them again, we can perform even better, doing what we need to do.

If we've been unfortunate enough to pick up an injury of our own and are out of action, we've got to dig deep. We got to accept the situation and focus on looking forward to making improvements. Once we get the momentum going, we progress as quickly as possible to get back to full fitness. We push to get back on the bike, back to where we were and then beyond where we were, getting better, fitter and stronger than before.

We regularly have to revisit the scene of a major moment or an "off" and we have to shake off the subversive memories. We have to slide the concerns to one side time and again until the bad memories fade and are replaced with new ones of success and triumph.

All the while we're persevering, we're being driven by a vision of those peak moments of doing what we love to the best of our ability.

Interestingly, some of the latest neuroscientific research is showing that when people do something they don't want to, a brain structure called the anterior midcingulate cortex gets bigger. This area is found to be larger in athletes and grows when people diet or overcome challenges. It's also been found that it remains larger in people who live a long time. It is being seen as potentially the seat of willpower and possibly even the will to live. Remember when I joked that mountain biking was the elixir for eternal youth?.. #justsayin'.

As well as developing resilience, we are constantly calling on our reservoirs of resourcefulness. We often have to figure out how to overcome logistical, navigational and mechanical problems on the fly. Sometimes our resources don't match the demands of the challenges we face and we have to improvise, adapt and overcome.

Our boundless innovation with cable ties, repurposed spares and another unsung hero "duct tape" is a testament to our resourcefulness. A mate of mine stands by the adage that, "If it can't be duct, it's f****d!"

Another mate put all these qualities to good use when he put a considerable gash in his thigh at Antur Stiniog. It happened just before lunch and whilst it didn't bleed much, it looked like it needed a fair number of stitches. He pottered off to his van to decide what to do. When he came back, and to our surprise, he presented a heavily duct-taped leg and declared he was going to stay and ride for the afternoon. "I reckon that'll be reet," he said.

Resilience, grit, resourcefulness, self-sufficiency and a sprinkling of madness perhaps?.. Actually, that might *also* be a by-product of MTB.

*Just for the record... I'm not condoning the above as an advisable course of self-care action. Please seek the advice of a doctor or healthcare professional if in any doubt about your health. *winky face**

Sometimes help isn't readily at hand though. There are situations when we need to be prepared and ready to be as self-sufficient as we can. We're often in the back of beyond, sometimes alone and the more conditioned we are the better.

Regardless of where we are or what we're doing, these skills and attributes along with good planning and preparation help us keep living well, riding hard, having maximum fun and enjoying life.

22 - Finale Ligure

I'd heard tales of a mythical land, a magical temperate place where trails lace the mountains like linguine – a region where endless ribbons of sumptuous single-track, skip high above stunning Mediterranean coastline and dive into juicy fruit-filled valleys. An area where you bob and weave past smallholdings, blast through olive groves and shred down dusty trails before filtering back through ancient Italian villages to bustling seaside towns with sandy beaches and enticing waters.

Legend had it that you could start the day being shuttled high into forested peaks, then spend the rest of it exploring hundreds of kilometres of tantalising trails, set in sublime scenery with breathtaking vistas.

Those days would be fuelled by the finest Italian coffee, fresh pasta and delicious gelato, furnished by the friendliest of folk. The icing on the brioche would be peeling off sweaty bike gear at the end of the day and diving into the crystal-clear waters of the Med. Follow that up with a snooze in the sun, frosty cold beers, palm-lined promenades, picturesque piazzas and perfect pizza.

Sounds pretty flippin' good eh?

But this isn't legend and it wasn't a myth. It's a real place and it does exist. *"Is-a called-a Finale Ligure and is-a bellissimo!"*

Actually, you probably already know about it. It's pretty well known. It's another MTB Mecca in Italy, on the Mediterranean coast between Genoa and Monaco.

Unsurprisingly, it's a favourite with bike mags, reviewers and content creators. The race format formerly known as Enduro World Series (EWS), now known as Enduro World Cup is a regular visitor to the region and it's also renowned for a monster 24-hour mountain bike race.

Still, knowing about it and hearing the stories is one thing but checking it out for yourself is something else.

I'm particularly partial to a portion of Italy anyway. They pretty much had me at pizza and pasta sealed the deal. The mental picture I'd already formulated about the place meant I was only ever going to need *zero* convincing to head off on a road trip to check it out for myself. I just needed the magic combo of free time and timing to fall into place to make it happen.

The stars eventually aligned and it looked like four of us might be headed off in mid-May for a long weekend of pre-season, spring riding. There'd be me, Jacko (you guessed it!) and a couple of other lads. One of them had been quite a few times and apparently had excellent knowledge of the trails, which would be very useful.

A guide is often recommended in the Finale region as the distances can be large, and navigational mistakes in the dense woodland can be costly. As well as avoiding getting lost, professional knowledge can really elevate your experience.

It wasn't long though before four became three. Then, as we got nearer to the trip, three became two and we'd lost our main "guide". It was just Jacko and me now. He'd been before and was fairly confident that he'd be fine finding his way around but I like having my own idea of where I am and what's going on, so I cracked on with a little bit of research of my own.

As part of my Proper Planning, Peter Piper Picked a Peck of Pickled Peppers, I pored over Google Maps, photos, YouTube, blogs and posts getting a feel for the lay of the land and comparing it to the data on the FATMAP app. I also upgraded to the paid version of the app so that we could download maps and access them even if the signal coverage dropped out when we were out in the sticks.

We'd probably be out for hours at a time, away from bike shops and support so we also needed to take a decent selection of spares, tools and supplies just in case.

Jacko booked us into a campsite he'd been to before and when the weekend finally rolled around, we loaded up the van. With bikes, kit and camping gear on board, we set off on a Friday lunchtime for the shlep across France and Italy, the final destination… Finale… "*Fitting!*"

Several hours later, we rolled into Finale Ligure, drove through the town, followed the beachfront, and turned left alongside a river course and away from the coast. We headed a short way up the road towards Calvisio and rocked up at Camping Tahiti early in the evening.

Camping Tahiti is located to the north-eastern "Finalpia" end of town, just a short walk to restaurants and cafes in the centre and not far from the public beach. It also operates its own bike up-lift shuttle-bus service, so we checked in, bought a big ol' trail map and booked morning uplifts for the following three days.

The campsite is located on the side of a hill and is arranged over a series of terraces. Our platform was about halfway up with a lovely view and just above the toilet block which we thought was very handy. We pitched our camp and headed out for some fresh fish and pasta. We hit the sack nice and early so that we'd be raring to go the following morning.

Finale is situated in the Ligurian Alps which hug the curve of the Italian coast. This is where the crook at the top of Italy's "boot" curls over to the west. It's a mountainous, forested region and if you've ever travelled across it, it can feel like a never-ending cycle of tunnel, bridge, tunnel, bridge, tunnel, bridge as the roads and train tracks split the elevation difference and pierce through the middle.

Valleys branch back from the coastline into the mountains and the town of Finale Ligure nestles at the end of one of them, where the Pora River meets the Ligurian Sea. To the south-west of the town, an imposing ridge rises abruptly from the water and then flanks the west of the river valley. It continues a gradual ascent inland in a north-westerly direction, first up to the village of Gorra and then on to Melogno above, and beyond.

A road called the Strada Provinciale 490 climbs from sea level and follows the rise of the ridge for 16 km, to elevations over 1000 m near Melogno.

Melogno is one of two main drop-off and start points for the main bike trails above Finale Ligure. It takes about 30 minutes to get there by shuttle bus and gives immediate access to the ever-popular and aptly named Roller Coaster.

At Melogno, the road splits and the right fork follows the ridge away to the east. It traces a horseshoe above the same valley below and to the right. Ten minutes later the road arrives at the second main drop-off/start point in the area, "NATO Base", which is, unsurprisingly, an ex-NATO base.

These two departure points can set you up for hours and hours of varied riding to get back to town. You can be back in just an hour or two if you crack on and take the direct route. Or, if you want to pedal, climb and explore more trails, you can easily turn it into a full day out.

We were woken early on Saturday morning by noisy German voices which took the edge off our "handy" proximity to the toilet block. Not to worry though, they were obviously excited (and oblivious) and we were too. We managed to doze off for a little while longer before dragging our backsides out of bed and getting ready.

Roller Coaster is probably the poster child track for the Finale region so we decided we'd do that first. We met the shuttle driver near reception, passed our bikes up into the back of his van, and then jumped in the front with three other guys.

We set off through Finale Ligure and back the way we'd come the night before. The driver joined the SP490, started to climb and chatted away merrily as he wound on and up into the mountains. They were looking decidedly damp, chilly and "gorillas in the mist" style as the warmth of the morning sun lifted gallons of moisture from the ground and back into the atmosphere, cooling it significantly.

Thirty minutes later, we pulled up in the small parking area at the Melogno T junction. There were a bunch of other shuttle vans, bikes and riders there already and the Osteria del Din restaurant across the road was doing a roaring trade with riders fuelling up on coffee and snacks.

We offloaded our bikes, thanked the driver but didn't set off for Roller Coaster... Jacko had remembered an extra bit that involved pedalling along the road and climbing a bit higher for a small bonus loop. I'd have skipped that if I was on my own but Jacko likes a pedal so, "Yeah mate, whatever. I'm easy."

A little while later, after a steep technically challenging climb/push and a fun natural, blue descent called Din, we popped back out on the same road and pedalled back along to Osteria del Din... Roller Coaster time!

You know when you're on an actual roller coaster and there's a bit near the start where you have to chug slowly up a hill? Yeah, well there's one of those on this one too that I hadn't been expecting. This day had already started off with a chunk more climbing than I'd been prepared for but after that... It was game on!

Roller Coaster deserved its label with some of it fitting the description to an absolute tee – 7 km of varied woodland flow trail, weaving, winding, swooping and soaring through the forest. Not too steep, not too mental but with plenty of fast sweeping turns, rolling bends and a few rock drops and jumps thrown into the mix.

The trees hug the trail, seemingly leaning in and whizzing past your head. A sensation that slaps me straight into *Return of the Jedi* on a speeder bike every time.

Some sections needed a few pedal cranks and there were a few segments where the turns tightened abruptly and set our tyres skittering and scrabbling as we desperately tried to shed speed to make the corners.

The trees and the undergrowth obscured the wider views most of the time but sometimes we could see we were on the top of the ridge as the ground rolled away to each side. From time to time we'd blast into or past a clearing where our field of view would expand across the valleys to other ridges and mountain peaks in the distance. The sun was winning its wrestling match with the morning moisture and clearing it away to reveal those spectacular, far-reaching views.

We popped out onto a small tarmac road, dog-legged along it to the right and dropped back into a steeper and rougher section. From time to time the limestone bedrock would give way to deeper orange sandstone, changing the colour, texture and characteristics of the trail. I didn't stop to check but it felt like the foliage changed too.

We finally popped out at the end of the trail and stopped beside a weathered-looking church called San Pantaleo. It was back on the SP490 and we paused to rehydrate, regroup and plan our next move.

After consulting the map and FATMAP, we decided that we'd carry on following the line of the ridge and explore that imposing lump at its base. The lump is the one that rose straight out of the sea beside Finale Ligure. It's called Monte Caprazoppa and is home to another network of trails.

A welcome, smooth, high-speed roll down the main road took us to the village of Gorra. The pastel colours of the houses looked like someone had tipped out a giant box of Edinburgh rock and stacked them alongside the road. More climbing followed and we scratched and scrabbled our way up from Gorra and back into the woods. We eventually found a purple (red equivalent) cross-country trail called Bondi.

This area proved more challenging in the navigation department, with little paths and trails shooting off and crisscrossing all over the place. We wouldn't have any problem finding our way back down to Finale one way or another but we wanted to ride the blue X-men so we kept stopping to check we were on the right track.

It felt like the limestone in this area had been on steroids. Knotted and gnarled lumps of it clawed out from the ground and the banks, threatening to brutally stub a toe or catch a pedal if your concentration lapsed.

When we eventually found X-men, it delivered the goods, big time! It kicked off with a series of berms, leading to sharper switchbacks and with the odd, rock-drop tossed into the mix. It was fast, loose and a lot of fun. There were also a few breathtaking viewpoints, looking out across Finale Ligure with the deep blue Mediterranean expanding to the right and the forested mountains, valleys and villages stretching inland to the left.

A couple of extra-sketchy, rocky, technical sections nearer the bottom wrapped things up for us with a nail-biting, final flourish. We popped back out onto a track and rejoined the main road at the south-western end of Finale Ligure.

We were ready for a snack as we rolled back through Finale and Jacko led us straight to a famous Focaccia shop which has a selection of variations on the theme. We bagged a couple each and ate them on a bench in the street before rolling on to his favourite Gelato shop for a couple of scoops of Italy's finest.

We headed back to camp, grabbed our swimmers and pedalled back to the beach for that dip in the sea and a snooze on the beach. Get in! To my surprise, the sea was even warm enough for a lengthy float!

So far, dare I say it, Finale was surpassing my expectations. This was just like the picture I'd had in my head. It was delivering big time and we were ticking things off the Italian/Finale to-do list like nobody's business.

I'd chosen the fresh fish and pasta option for last night's dinner and Jacko had a request for tonight's.

He'd already delivered on the trails, the focaccia and the gelato.

Which Italian delight was he going to come up with next?

What little hidden gem was he going to unearth this time?

Curry.

Haha! Yep curry. He'd clocked an Indian restaurant in town and that's what he fancied, "Haha! Yeah, whatever, I'm easy mate." and to be fair, it was pretty damn good.

Up and at 'em on day two! It kicked off with a very entertaining episode for me, as Jacko tried to extract a scary-looking scorpion (*"As opposed to a not scary-looking scorpion?.."*) that had moved into his tent. *"Yikes!"* I was well pleased I was in the roof of the van.

Next stop, shuttle bus – Same time, same dude, same bus, different compadres, different destination.

We dropped the other guys at Melogno and stayed on board for NATO Base or "Bass NATO" as it's pronounced in Italian. The van dropped us a little way short on a large concrete slab drop-off area. We pedalled up the hill with a whole bunch of other riders from different shuttles to NATO Base itself. More concrete slabs and a collection of concrete structures – abandoned and empty but now emblazoned and transformed from their utilitarian military origins with some fantastic brightly coloured graffiti.

We climbed up a steep, stoney track into the woods to find the entrance to a blue trail called Crestino. That would continue sweeping along the ridge before peeling right into a purple trail called "Ingegnere". This is another well-known one in the area and another fast fun lengthy descent.

Ingegnere starts out as flowy winding single-track. It's a narrow track to start off with as it flows through the woods but it slowly and steadily turns up the heat as you tick off the kilometres. Before you know it, you're hurtling down narrow rocky canyons, with the periphery blurring on a white-knuckle ride. Big fun!

We popped out of the bottom onto a single-lane road and chattered away, excitedly reminiscing as we sped along. The gradient levelled then reversed and we began to climb. We knew where we were aiming for today and we knew we had a bit of a pedal to get there.

We were hot and hungry and we agreed that if we found somewhere that looked nice we'd stop and grab a bite to eat rather than snacking on the fly.

Ask and Ye Shall Receive!... Within a few minutes, we pedalled into a little village called Feglino and immediately heard the sound of voices, laughter and good times. As I tuned my ears to locate the source, Jacko said, "Look, that says *Mountain Bikers Set Menu.*" There was a big sign right next to us for a restaurant called Aspettando il Sole.

We tiptoed down a steep cobbled path and peeped around a corner to find a small enclosed terrace, shaded by a vine entwined pergola. There sat maybe five large tables full of fellow mountain bikers, chatting away and tucking into some delicious-looking grub. "*Get in!*"

We dumped our bikes and asked the lady for a table. There were none left outside so we shimmied past the tables of Italian, German, Dutch, English and American voices and headed inside to a traditional old Italian building and sat down.

A couple of massive Newfoundland dogs were padding lazily around inside. The lady took our drinks order but nothing else and within a minute they arrived. They were swiftly followed by a couple of plates and a big dish of food, barley mainly (I think) with peppers, green beans and a tasty sauce. "This must be a starter," we agreed, so we halved it onto our plates and got stuck in. It was delicious!

Then some bread arrived... "Grazie" we chorused... Then cured salami and focaccia... Then a bowl of broad bean pods... Then some spinach pastries and salad... Wow! I'd already seen people tucking into big plates of pasta outside, so if this *was* a set menu, there was still plenty more to come!

Everything that landed on our table was delicious, and the whole venue felt like a hidden gem you might see on a foodie TV travel show. It seemed to be family-run and there were stunning views across the valley to put the cherry on top. It was exactly the kind of experience I dream of.

We made a considerable dent in the "starter" before conceding defeat. The plates disappeared and the pasta arrived, coated in a creamy pesto sauce with a bowl of Parmesan on the side. Holy moly! Our afternoon on the bikes could be a bit of a challenge after all this!

Chocolate mousse, cream and espressos finished things up and we parted with a reasonable 18€ each for the pleasure. We thanked the ladies heartily and pedalled slowly away from the restaurant and very tentatively uphill for the next half an hour. Everything settled surprisingly well actually… These guys know what they're doing.

We were heading for another mountain plateau which separated us from our campsite and the coast by about 3 km as the crow flies. This table of peaks also had its own network of trails streaked all over the top and dribbling down the sides.

We carried on towards a town called Orco and could see a band of climbing cliffs heralding our way towards Monte Cucco. We rode on until we found a campsite called Base Camp Cucco. A green trail called Cucco (there's a theme developing here!) started here and would lead us up, into hills and away from civilisation once again. Cucco proved to be an undulating cross-country trail that led us around the flank of Cucco itself and the plateau. This area was labelled as the San Bernadino area on our map. We eventually veered left and climbed to the summit of the plateau making our way towards Monte Tolla at its southern end. We were attempting to find our way to a purple trail called Megalithic which would link into a blue trail called Ca del Vacchè.

Like the Monte Caprazoppa area the day before, this area needed a bit more attention with the navigation, just to make sure. It wasn't always obvious which way a junction or a fork went and we did have to backtrack a couple of times to get back on the right track.

Megalithic started out on limestone pavement with thick bush foliage and as the trail rolled over towards the valley and the gradient increased, the gnarled limestone territory returned. Blasting through thick woodland alongside man-made limestone terraces and channels felt like we were exploring some ancient structures abandoned by mankind and reclaimed by nature. (*"Der! It's literally called megalithic dumbass!"*) The trail seamlessly transitioned into Ca del Vacchè at some point, and before long the structures were inhabited again and we were ducking through archways and between buildings on our final approach to the village of Calvisio.

This was just up the river valley at our end of town so we pedalled back along the river to our camp and fell straight into our new routine.

Gelato – beach – swim – snooze – showers – beer (not for Jacko) – pizza – bed. Mint!

We'd be travelling back home on day three but we still wanted to ride before we set off in the afternoon. We had something a bit more concise planned for the morning.

We went through the same shuttle rigmarole, hopped off at Melogno and set off down Roller Coaster. It was even better the second time around with a little extra familiarity. We had a better idea of where to send it, where to gap, where to let fly and maybe even more importantly, where not to.

On Saturday, we'd popped out on a tarmac track towards the bottom of the trail and dog-legged right for the final section. This time, we turned left and pedalled out along the tarmac track for a short distance to find a different church. This one is called Madonna della Guardia. It marks the start point for a couple of trails that would drop us into the valley at Calice Ligure and upriver from Finale. It would also give us a chance to ride a couple of trails that were on our wish list for the weekend, the purple Kill Bill 1 and our final trail of the trip, and the first black of the weekend, Madonna della Guardia… *"Wait. Hold on a minute. Ahaa!"*

Kill Bill 1 had another undulating, swooping, swerving roller coaster feel to it. It was punctuated by rollovers that were a touch steeper than you'd anticipated when you'd already committed to the roll-in. A few big compressions and tightening corners almost caught me off guard. On first ride, there were places where the flow stalled a bit but it felt like a few laps and getting to know this bad boy would be a lot of fun.

It meandered on, swerving between the trees and then the gorse bushes again. We eventually popped out on a track and had to check back in with FATMAP to recalibrate for the entrance of Madonna... so to speak.

We found the entrance and paused for a moment to catch our breath and guzzle some water. Madonna started out with a lengthy high-speed traverse to the right, between the trees and bushes, and along what felt like a terrace.

As it progressed, it turned out to be another one that gradually turns up the heat. It steadily cranks up the intensity, until you are blowing out of your backside and hanging on for dear life. It'll let up for a moment, lulling you into a false sense of security, inviting you in, then it dials up the volume and increases the gnar.

It's rocky, steep, rough and dusty. Sections feel like the Canyon in Les Gets where you end up in a channel of rock with banks whizzing past at head height and increasing the sensation of speed.

Just when you think you're getting the measure of it, it throws in a rock garden of epic proportions. A huge chunk of monolithic sloping, striated rock, with ridges and hollows sloping down and to the left. It intimidates you aggressively as you barrel your way through, praying that it doesn't tuck your front wheel and dump you violently onto the ground.

We both went in way too hot and the only option was to dig deep and see it through.

Then it's over! It dialled all the way up to 11 and then *boom!* It's over.

There'd been plenty more than one occasion where I'd had a nervous little chuckle to myself on this descent. It's an awesome trail and certainly felt like it deserved its billing as the most technical trail in Finale.

And what a finale in Finale!

We pedalled merrily along the road in the valley bottom back towards Finale Ligure. Approaching from this side meant we'd be arriving at the Finalborgo end of town. It's a medieval hamlet of Finale Ligure dating back to the end of the 12th century. We pedalled and pushed through the narrow streets until we found a characterful and quintessentially Italian cafe bar for a tasty espresso and a fitting bookend to our Finale trip.

We headed back to the van at the campsite, loaded up and shipped out… Home time!

Well… I'd heard tales of a mythical land and they certainly weren't "tall" tales, and, it definitely wasn't mythical. Expectations had been high, but Finale had delivered on all of them.

The trails were terrific and they are constantly being improved and adjusted. A little bit of Italy is always a treat and funnelling down to the sea for a dip at the end of each day just adds an extra special dimension.

The paper map and FATMAP combo had proved a winner for us but we'd barely scratched the surface. I've got another mate from Torico bike shop in Morzine who's been going for many years. He regularly gets a guide and always comes back astonished by the extent of new and varied trails that stretch way back into the mountains.

Finale had been so good that I got home chatted to the fam' and booked to go again a couple of weeks later!.. We had a long bank holiday weekend coming up so I went back with Nina and the kids! I'm all excited again just writing this. It's been a while and I might just even have to look at booking another little, cheeky something in a minute.

Bellissimo! Grazie Mille Finale!

23 - Connection to Nature

There are more of us humans on planet Earth than ever before, over 8 billion at the last count. As a species, we push back and cover up the natural world to make way for our homes, businesses, organisations, towns and cities.

Over half of the world's population now live in cities and urban areas and many people inadvertently spend more and more time inside, increasingly insulated from the natural world.

That disconnect can be exacerbated by the abundance of information, resources and entertainment we have at our fingertips. We are blessed with an astonishing array of digital tools but they can pull our attention and awareness away from the physical world almost completely.

We know though, that getting out there and spending time reconnecting with nature is super good for us. There is overwhelming evidence that it's beneficial in so many ways.

It's not surprising... We are nature. We're not separate from it, but a part of something that we've been evolving with for millennia. We're made of the same primary elements as everything else and we're imbibed with the same life force that's flowing through the rest of Earth's living system. We're inextricably linked. Essentially, we're its "wickle" (little) babies. "*Aww.*"

I don't know if evidence or rationale is even necessary. All you've got to do is go for a walk on a beach, through the woods, sit beside a river, feel the wind in your hair or the sun on your face and it just feels right.

It's easy to forget those feelings when you're inside and plugged in but when you get out there, it comes rushing straight back, *"Oo yeah… That's the ticket."*

Now, don't get me wrong, I enjoy visiting a city once in a while, and some of them are amazing, but after two or three days, I'm getting twitchy. I'm usually starting to feel slightly hemmed-in and ready to beat a retreat back to the sticks for a fix of space, mountain air and "wilderness".

I'm also not averse to a bit of digital absorption either. I'll happily plug in and disconnect with the best of them but I've learned from personal experience that for me, too much disconnect is not optimal. It's all about the balance.

This is where, once again, mountain biking is awesome… It's an excellent facilitator to draw us out regularly into the natural environment. *"Doo it, doo it"* gets to work and before we know it, we're back out there, getting a dose of the tonic. Not only does it act as a catalyst to get us out there in the first place, but it coaxes us into an ever-deepening connection with our natural world.

We've talked about mudding, grounding, forest bathing and the intimate knowledge we build of the surface of our fabulous planet, but mountain biking helps us tune into the flow and cadence of the natural world.

We observe the rhythms of the seasons more closely, recognising their transitions with greater awareness. Not just in a clunky spring-to-summer, autumn-to-winter kind of way but by appreciating the fine gradual blend of changes that take place as we wobble, whirl and whoosh around the sun.

We watch as the fresh green shoots of spring unfurl and blossom into a cacophony of colour and life. We hear the arrival of insects, bugs and birds, multiplying in the juiciest of green worlds. We feel the brightness of the sun strobing through the dark shade of full trees as we blast down the trails.

We watch that vibrant green gradually fade as the strength of the sun's rays increases. We see and hear the bursts of insect life after the return of the rain and watch their numbers lazily dwindle as the dry heat returns. We feel the change in the air and watch the shadows lengthen as the days shorten, the leaves, turn and the fungi fruit.

Those turning leaves ripen and glow before finally losing the strength to hold on. They cascade down around us, coating the ground with a whole new riding surface and a whole different set of sensations. Eventually, the tentacles of winter's chill reach into our world and the days' contract. Frost begins to line the early morning trails. Nature slows and rests, ready and waiting as always for the curtain call and the next performance.

We watch, wait and look forward to our own personal, favourite riding windows, those times of the year when the conditions, the surroundings and the weather seem to align with something that just clicks deep within us.

We even begin to notice the hiccups, glitches and minor changes. We notice the false starts to a season, early starts, late starts and different characteristics from year to year.

We keep an eye on the weather patterns and learn how the meteorological nuances affect the trails we ride, our riding itself and how we prepare.

We become aware of the smaller cycles and changes throughout the day from the frost, dew or deep blue skies of the mornings to dusty, dry, hazy afternoons. We learn how the ground dries, how it drains and how it absorbs.

We don't just observe though; we are immersed. We are out there. We're *in it*, absorbing the ambience, exposed to everything the weather throws at us. Our senses are fired, reinforcing our connection and increasing our awareness of those cycles, rhythms and patterns.

We disappear into seas of green, blasting across meadows and fields and merging into the woodland theatre. We're surrounded by an abundance of life, flora, fauna and fungi. The sights, smells and the sounds, the sensations and the ambience. The rain, the cloud, the sun, the wind and the snow. There's so much to experience especially when you remember to pause and drink it all in.

These experiences are obviously different for riders around the world but whatever the local, natural characteristics, the essence of the experience and connection is the same.

Harmonising with our natural environment is not just beneficial to our riding but is an absolute pleasure in itself. As we build our connection, our appreciation increases, our love for it deepens and our respect is strengthened... And that surely is a good thing for us and it.

24 - World Champs, Les Gets 2022

Some people like watching football, some like watching cricket, rugby, tennis, kabaddi, whatever. Each to their own, and they're all great in their own right, but if you're anything like me, nothing quite compares to downhill mountain bike racing. For me, that right there, that is the absolute nectar.

Watching the top, elite, downhill riders doing battle, to see who can hurtle down a bonkers track, on the side of a mountain, in the shortest amount of time possible... What's not to love?

Watching on TV is all well and good but the spectacle and atmosphere in the flesh are something else. Especially in Les Gets!

It's the skill on display, the bravery, the risk. It's edge-of-your-seat excitement, slipping, sliding and scrabbling around in the woods. It's the fact you can actually ride a lot of the same tracks and experience just how insane the level is, for the top pilots to do what they do.

By the start of last summer, we'd already had the immense privilege and pleasure of witnessing three Crankworx events and two MTB World Cups, but 2022 was going to be even bigger.

2022 would be the "Big Kahuna", the "Mac-Daddy", the "Don Mega"... The Mountain Bike World Championships were coming to town!

If you're not already familiar with the Mountain Bike World Cup and World Champs, they are both annual events sanctioned by the Swiss-based Union Cycliste Internationale, more commonly known as the UCI.

The World Cup or "World Series" consists of several World Cup race stops at various venues around the world. Riders compete for the top spot at each one. The points accumulated from each race decide the overall World Cup winners at the end of the season.

The World Championships on the other hand is once a year. It is one-day, one-run, one-chance, all-or-nothing, no-holds-barred, balls-out madness. It's held at a different venue every year and the riders are selected by and primarily represent their home countries ahead of their usual race teams. The winners of the different disciplines and classes are crowned World Champions and get to wear the coveted rainbow-striped jersey until the next World Champs.

These competitions are held for all sorts of cycling disciplines but Les Gets had been and would be hosting the Cross Country (XC) Short Circuit races and the XC Marathon. That was as well as the one that's going to get the big love right here, the Downhill.

I'm going to issue a quick note to the XC fans and riders. These guys and girls do an awesome job. Their physical prowess and riding skills are off the chart and the races are a spectacle to behold. As we've already established though,

DH is what gets my juices fizzing so that's where I'm going with this one. Big respect nonetheless!

Teams, organisers, sponsors, brands and volunteers arrive at the start of the week and take over the town for several days of mayhem. Every spare, square inch of tarmac gets sprayed up with team designations in advance. The night before they arrive, the local tow trucks get to work shipping out any straggler cars whose owners haven't taken the "no-parking" notifications seriously.

The trucks and vans begin to roll in, tents are erected and the travelling circus sprouts up like expanding foam filling all the nooks and crannies of the village.

Les Gets is an awesome venue for this event because the town itself sits high on a col, with views down into the valleys on either side to the east and west. You've then got mountain slopes stretching upwards to the north and south.

The XC races take place on the north-facing slopes on the south side of town and the Downhill is held on the south face of Mont Chéry on the north side of town. It's probably only a two-minute walk from the finish line of one to the finish line of the other.

Each discipline can get busy doing their things in their own arena but all the tracks, competitors, spectators and super-charged energy ultimately flow back down to the finish areas. Everything converges in town making for an awesome atmosphere throughout the whole week. Combine that with oodles of accommodation and hospitality for all tastes and it's nigh-on a match made in heaven.

After an 18-year hiatus, this was going to be a big one for Les Gets. The last time the World Champs had been here was back in 2004. That was one for the history books as well. Back then, Steve Peat's blistering race run, as well as his hopes of a maiden World Champs, were dashed in a cloud of dust, when he binned it within sight of the finish line.

Frenchman, Fabien Barel took the title on that day. He was on home turf, surrounded by his countrymen and part of a roster littered with even more names that would go on to be legends on two wheels; Greg Minnaar took the silver medal, Sam Hill bronze and Nico Vink was in the mix.

In 2022 there was yet another quiver of top French riders vying for their chance of home glory. Big dogs like Loïc Bruni, Amaury Pierron, Loris Vergier and Myriam Nicole were perhaps the most well known of an ever-competitive conveyor belt of French mountain bike talent. A raft of riders from GB, Europe, the US, Australia, New Zealand and across the world were out to deny them and claim glory for themselves.

The gravity, intensity and one-day, one-shot nature of this event regularly draw even larger crowds than the World Cup races. Since it had last been held in Les Gets, and with the renewed profile from the 2019 and 2021 World Cups, no one knew quite what to expect, but most probably, a shed-load of people and a magnificent spectacle!

We had friends visiting from the UK that week and we spent much of it catching up with them, riding, mooching around the pits, watching practice/qualifying sessions and soaking up the atmosphere.

The anticipation was building. A hot, toasty day with blazing sun and dusty trails was on the cards. The riders were waxing lyrical about how good the track was. *"Bring it on!"*

When race day rolled around, Pauline Ferrand-Prévot had bagged a win in the women's XC short track the night before, so the Frenchies were already buzzing.

Unfortunately, Nina and Izzy wouldn't be joining us because *fortunately*, Izzy had qualified for a national swimming comp down south. *Unfortunately*, Thomas and I would miss Izzy racing but *fortunately*, we had the World Championships to watch instead.

The rest of us met up and headed into town. It immediately became apparent that this was indeed going to be a big one! In true French style, there were cars parked everywhere and squished into every available space. The main road through Les Gets was almost at a standstill and things were so tight that even the motorbikes were unable to filter past the stalled traffic.

We strode quickly by on foot, which was by far the fastest mode of transport, and headed for Mont Chéry lift station. The plan, as usual for a Chéry downhill race, was to head to the top of Mont Chéry and walk down alongside the track. We could catch the action all the way down, before coinciding our arrival near the finish area with that of top 10 qualifiers, one of whom would most likely be crowned champ.

As we got closer to Mont Chéry the cause of the traffic hold-up became clear... *People!..* Thousands of them, and at 11.00 am the party was already in full effect.

The queue for the lift was already a hundred metres long and as we filed to the back of it, we passed air horns, vuvuzelas, chainsaw engines, fancy dress, crates of beer and bulk boxes of wine adapted into portable, boozy backpacks.

Some of the people passing through in the vehicles on the road looked completely shell-shocked. The mob swirled down the road rhythmically engulfing and releasing them as they went. Many were there to join the party as well and got busy blasting their horns to add to the bedlam.

The atmosphere was bonkers! There was plenty of good-hearted banter flying around, especially when random civilians on bikes rode past and were cheered on with a deafening wave of World Championship level support.

We eventually shuffled our way up the steps to the Mont Chéry télécabine, filed through the turnstiles and clambered into one of the "white eggs" to be whisked up to the mid-station. Phew!

When you step out of the lift station on Mont Chéry and wander around to the front of Le Belvédère restaurant, you are greeted by a panoramic view that is just a little bit special. On a clear sunny summer's day, the bustling alpine village of

Les Gets nestles in the valley bottom below. As your gaze climbs, it scans over the juicy green, trail-laced slopes, it's led over patches of woodland to rocky mountainous peaks and the majestic Mont Blanc massive towering beyond.

On a day like that one, deep dark blue skies crown the spectacle lending the perfect contrast to the timber chalets at the base, the greens, the greys and the brilliant white of the snow on the tops in the distance.

The panorama stretches from Nantaux in the west, tracking over Mossettes, Avoriaz, Haut Fort, the Dents du Midi beyond, Dent Blanche, the top of the Pleney lift in Morzine, Pointe de Nyon, Angolon, Chamossière, the Mont Blanc Massif, Flaine and the Grand Massif, Pointe Percy and finally, Pointe de Marcelly away to the east. Abso-freakin-lutely stupendous.

This list of names might mean nothing to you right now but if you even come for a visit, you might want to know then, and it really is a special view. Even better with a cold beverage in the sunshine and a spot of lunch on Belvédère's Terrace but not today! We were on a mission.

We soaked the view up nonetheless and wandered across to the Pointe chairlift for the second leg of our journey to the summit. The Pointe chairlift is an old-school one and can be a vicious little bugger. It's one of those chairs that comes in fast, takes you by surprise and cracks you hard in the calf as it does. Then, as you are dumped wincing into the seat, it gives you the old "one-two" with a dig to the spine on its un-cushioned, metal-bar, back-support.

To be fair, the lifties usually do a great job of taking the sting out of it, by physically wrestling that bad boy into submission, but I don't take any chances now. I always make sure to reach back with a hand to contribute to the lift-chair wrangling.

It's a fine high-altitude ride on the Pointe chair and as we ascended, we eventually peeped over the crest that was blocking the top of the WC track from our view lower down. We could now see the last of the riders dropping in from the start hut for final practice. They'd drop in, accelerating through the first few berms, send the first step-down, rocket off across the traverse, gap the track without missing a beat and fire off into the foliage. *"Man, do they charge!"*

We scuttled awkwardly off the lift as it came in low to the rubber-matted landing and bid, "Merci" ("Thank you") and "Bonne journée" ("Have a good day") to the lifty at the top.

The summit is only another 50 yards or so and we hiked up for an even more epic view than beside Belvédère – one which stretched the full 360 degrees.

It was now time to get up close and personal with some hard race action for the next few hours.

The seven of us slid and skidded our way down dusty, gravely tracks and slippy grassy slopes, peppered with myrtille (blueberry) bushes to the start hut. This was a nice little teaser for our guests in terms of what their day held in store.

We were bang on time for the start of the Elite Women's final at 1.15 pm and by my reckoning, we had about three hours now to get down to the bottom and catch the last 10 men coming through the finish line.

The women started firing out of the start hut one by one on their beeline for the base of Mont Chéry. We set off too, at a slightly slower pace, and spent the next three hours slipping, sliding and scrabbling our way down the sides of the DH course.

We traversed back and forth across the track at the crossing points along the way. We'd pause to watch the nutty feats of skill and bravery at fan hotspots like the "Les Gets Road Gap". Not a small gap by any means and made even sketchier by the immediate left-hand corner to deal with, after landing at full chat. At least the course builders had made the berm a bit more substantial this year, and they'd taken out the tree that was positioned scarily on the outside of the corner.

We teetered and wound down through the woods. We'd stop as the cascade of whistles and cheers crescendoed towards us as each rider approached. We'd cheer them past, then crane to see them and the wave of support ripple down the hill and out of sight.

Camille Balanche whizzed past as the last of the women and a few minutes later we got word that Austrian, Valentina

Höll had held on to the top spot and taken the title of World Champion for the women. Nina Hoffmann bagged the silver with Frenchwoman and previous World Champion Miriam Nicole being pipped into third and missing out on home turf glory.

About halfway down the track and back near the Belvédère, we stopped at the Fanzone. A giant screen had been erected above the reservoir for spectators to gather and watch. Les Gets Ski Club had set up a stand selling sandwiches, snacks, drinks and beer to raise money for the kids' training.

The stand was completely *mobbed* and the queue was massive. The plan was to grab lunch here but by the time we'd got to the front of the queue, all of the sandwiches and snacks had sold out. We'd have to make do with excitement and the calories from beer and fizzy pop to sustain us for the next few hours.

We pushed on down through the woods with hundreds of other spectators and passed hundreds more on their way up. We now had a constant companion of escalating noise. Marshals' whistles, horns, air horns, clapping, cheering, bike frames and rims being drummed with metal bars, and the more than occasional chainsaw engine.

The sweat from the heat of the day and the exertion of descending had formed a perfect catch-net for the fine dust that was in a constant state of suspension in the atmosphere. No sooner did gravity return a particle to Earth than another tyre or foot would sling it high in the air again. We'd gained a layer of bronze foundation that would fit right in on *The Only Way Is Essex*!

I was keeping an eye on the Red Bull coverage and live timings on my phone. I was attempting to keep up-to-date with all the action and make sure we were on track to get to the bottom at the right time. That wasn't proving easy because the reception was pretty pants. I supposed the local 4G antennas must have been buckling at the knees with the sheer volume of demand.

After the halfway point, the number of people hiking up increased, making things even more interesting. A highlight of the track walk for me, is the riders' right side of the track, at the last wood section christened "The Black Wood 2.0". This is just before the canyon gap where Reese Wilson did his infamous OTB (over the bars) superman crash in 2021. The gap had been re-christened "The Swan Dive" in honour of that.

It's extremely steep and dusty here, plus they'd logged it since last year meaning there were dust, roots, tree stumps, fallen trees and piles of branches everywhere. Hundreds of us were scrambling up and cascading down in the super-heated dust cloud. We'd all pause for grip to try and crane for a view and cheer when a rider blasted through.

I've seen many people take mega tumbles in this section but still manage to keep hold of their plastic glass full of beer. That always gets a cheer almost as big as a passing rider!

We walked the final leg past the "Straight Shooter" and the "Whip Stadium". We stopped to watch riders hurtle through and timed our arrival at the final corner perfectly. Ten riders remained as we filtered deep into an enormous, noisy and excitable crowd.

The decibel levels were soaring, not least from my little man, Thomas, who was now a permanent installation on my shoulders where he'd secured an excellent view. He seemed to have nailed circular breathing and was blowing his vuvuzela in an almost continuous stream of din.

One by one, the riders came in and we followed what we could on my phone, and from T's view of the big screen from his elevated position.

Aussie, Troy Brosnan came flying through and went P1.

Brit Laurie Greenland followed and slotted in P2.

Next came 40-year-old defending World Champ and previous four-time winner Gregg Minnaar who ended up in 7th place.

Andreas Kolb hit a tree on the way down but still managed 18th.

Ex 2x World Champ Danny Hart was off the pace after a big crash in practice during the week and came in at 20th.

There were now only five riders left to drop and four of them were French. Next up was the man most of the crowd would be rooting for, Loïc Bruni... Super-Bruni! He was carrying a shoulder injury but was already a four-time World Champion. If anyone could pull something out of the bag on the day, it was him.

The crowd went bananas as Bruni came through, railed the final berm, reached over the line and went green!.. P1!.. He'd gone a massive 3.9 seconds faster than Brosnan!

The crowd noise went through the roof! It felt like it was melting reality. It held for a couple of minutes then faded a little because it wasn't over yet.

With three Frenchmen left to drop, only Canadian Finn Iles could ruin the French party.

Benoît Coulanges came next and despite being the fastest qualifier, he had a few loose moments and only managed 8th.

Loris Vergier put in a clean and precise run and slotted into 2nd place behind Bruni.

We waited patiently for Finn Iles to drop; there seemed to be an extended delay and then it came over the speakers and the live feed that he wouldn't be starting. He'd had a massive crash in practice that morning, so big that it had destroyed his helmet and there had been a big question mark as to whether he would ride in the final.

A cheer went up around the crowd. Not for Finn's misfortune but with only Amaury Pierron left to descend, the French were now guaranteed another downhill World Champion on home turf.

If anyone was capable of nabbing the title from Bruni it was Pierron. He is a phenomenal rider and was enjoying a blistering World Cup season with four wins out of seven races.

The wave of noise followed him down the mountain and charged towards us. The crowd went absolutely crazy as he came past and as he thrust his bike forward across the line he went P2! Bruni had done it! Title number five, a French one, two, three and a podium lockout!

The crowd went nuts and started charging forward from our corner. This hadn't been intentional positioning but it was perfect. We weren't contained by the barriers here and could follow the surge with Thomas still on my shoulders straight down the track, under the finish arch and right into the middle of the mix in the finish enclosure.

Flares, smoke, noise, dust, chainsaws, horns, the clanking of metal on metal, excitement on the PA, absolute bedlam! We could see Loïc celebrating and being completely mobbed by fans, friends, colleagues, riders and anyone who could get near him.

When we watched this whole scene back on Red Bull TV the next day, Rob Warner said, "I have never, in my whole life, seen anything like that, and I've been at these races for 30 years. It's unbelievable!"

It was estimated that 70,000 people were in Les Gets on that Saturday for the downhill finals. Amazing!

The pandemonium didn't let up either and we absorbed every second for goodness knows how long. When it did begin to calm, we were ready for a beer and we headed to the Les Gets Vélo Club bar this time.

It was another fundraising venture for local club kids and this time set up in the base of the Mont Chéry lift station. Front row spectating for all the action in the finish area and beer on tap, not a bad venue for a volunteering gig. We spotted a few friends there and chatted excitedly while we got some drinks in.

Eventually, the celebrations started to creep towards the square in the centre of town where the podiums would be taking place. A fancy World Champs stage had been erected for the podiums, gigs, DJs and events that were on during the week.

Thousands of spectators converged in the square. The flow seemed never-ending and as people kept streaming in, some of them started clambering for a better view. We'd already got a good spot towards the back on a raised flower bed but people started climbing onto porches, balconies and roofs. It was total mayhem but absolutely brilliant! The Frenchies were doing spectating like they do parking. If there's a space and it is physically possible to get to it, it's game on!

Eventually, the organisers got around to the presentations and the women came out first with a massive cheer for Myriam Nicole, who was gracious but obviously disappointed. Hoffmann and Höll followed and received worthy applause. Then the men came out, were awarded their trophies and the place went completely ballistic!

What an experience! What an experience for Loïc who was visibly emotional. What an experience for Amaury and Loris, for the crowd, for the people watching on TV, and for us. Absolutely amazing!

There's a huddle of bars in the centre of town in Les Gets focused around Barbylone, Black Bear, Irish Bar, Bar Bowling and The Igloo nightclub. When there are a lot of people in town or an event is on, the whole street is closed. Pop-up bars, speakers and food stands spring up and the whole area transforms into party central. Tonight's would be going on well into the early hours and probably all night.

We wandered down to Barbylone in the centre for a couple more beers and saw my mate who runs it. This place would be a focal point for the celebrations and it would likely be mental. When we got there, he was sharing some chips with his partner and kids before they'd leave him to get down to business. As they left, his partner held him in a lengthy embrace and kissed him as if he was going off to battle and she may never see him again. This was going to be some serious partying!

We'd still not really eaten anything since breakfast and whilst the beers were going down well, they could do with a little something to help absorb them. The kids were getting a bit tired and hungry, and most of the group were ready to call it a day.

Some of us had major FOMO though and we talked a big game about walking all the way home, eating, regrouping and coming back down. Even though I wanted to, I suspected that once I was home, comfortable and the excitement started to subside, I wouldn't be arsed… I was right. We walked back thoroughly buzzing off the day's events, ate some food, showered a ton of dust off our bodies, hit the sack and game over. What a day!

25 - The Bikes

We've talked about the characters and the camaraderie, the tracks, the terrain and the travel. I've touched on the progression and the planning, the resilience, resourcefulness and the racing. I've waffled on about my experiences which I hope resonate with yours, but *OH MY DAYS… What about the bikes!?*

Oof!… MmmMmmMmm!.. *Bites 2nd knuckle on forefinger of balled fist*

The bikes are stunningly magnificent. They are marvels of modern engineering. They are the manifestations of imagination that allow our whole passion to even exist.

These things are designed and built solely to bring maximum efficiency and fun, in our quest to ride the world we live in, on two wheels, without limits, with maximum speed and unfettered expression.

It's amazing how far mountain bikes have come from their rigid ancestors with zero suspension and primitive rim brakes. We are now blessed with cutting-edge designs, geometry, materials and components.

Advanced suspension systems, track the terrain and iron out the roughest of ground. They provide support when we need it, pop on demand and absorb huge compressions when we drop from the heavens.

Drivetrains are efficient, smooth and fast. There an astonishing array of components to fit every individual preference and demand. Frames, wheels and bars resist phenomenal forces. The whole thing works in harmony with state-of-the-art braking systems, to deliver ferocious stopping power.

The bikes are works of art and technical genius. They are creations of practical performance. It's truly amazing that the manufacturers can design and build things that are so refined and precise, yet can withstand so much punishment.

It's not just about performance either. Well, it is but it isn't. It's always a bonus if something looks good as well as having a banging personality and there are so many glorious machines to ogle at. It's a pleasure checking out seductive bikes when you're out and about, surfing the web, or cruising the shops.

It's perfectly acceptable, appreciated even, to perv over other people's bikes when you're on the hill or in a lift queue. Beauty is in the eye of the beholder; we've all got our favourites and it's always funny when there's a collective turning of heads when something truly stunning speeds past.

Bike desire escalates to fever pitch when the pros are in town, with world-class designs and prototype tech on show. At the World Champs, in particular, the manufacturers, teams and mechanics go the extra mile with custom paint jobs and all kinds of other special one-off details.

It's a dangerous game letting your eyes wander though. Sometimes you're better off keeping the blinkers on. You let your head turn for a moment and the next thing, the desire creeps in… Before you know it, you've had a couple of drinks, remortgaged the house, handed over your cash and there's a hot new German model on its way.

All that research, design, development and engineering does come at a price though and some of those prices are eye-watering. Some terrific memes do the rounds and kind of hit the nail on the head:

My house
(Alongside a picture of a ramshackle old shed)

My Car
(Alongside a picture of an ageing rust bucket)

My Bike
(Alongside a picture of a 10K tricked-out carbon weapon. Haha!)

Or

"My biggest fear is dying…
And my wife finding out
how much I spent on bikes."

Or

"Teach your kids to love mountain bikes…

210

And they'll never have money for drugs."

-

If you do ever pull the trigger, new bike days are peak moments in life, like marriage or the birth of a child... Just kidding!.. Just kidding kids... Just kidding Nina...;D They are great though.

It is a bit like taking a new baby home. It doesn't live in the garage yet... Not that your new baby would, but your precious new arrival comes in the house for a few days, to be admired and fawned over, until it's taped up and ready for the outside world.

You feel an instinctive and innate desire to nurture it and keep it safe at all costs. You want to protect it from any potential damage or kidnappers and wonder whether it'd be weird if you set up a camp bed to sleep beside it, just in case.

It's wrapped and ready to go but two days later, it's still in the living room. You've got used to having it around and checking it out every time you pass by.

It's like a piece of art, but an interactive one, that you keep balancing on, bunny hopping around and wheeling three metres, leaving streaks of black rubber all over the flooring.

You also know though, that this is *the* most pristine state this thing will ever be in. It's in peak condition and it's a shame to even get those tyres dirty. Appreciate it while it lasts by all means but sooner or later you're ready to overcome the inertia and let that thing eat! Game on!

What many of these bikes can handle and the confidence they inspire is really quite astonishing. The engineers just continue upping the game, making more things possible, more things rideable and more things enjoyable.

I've dished out some love here and there in this book, but the designers, engineers, mechanics and others who produce and maintain these bikes and their components, deserve a special slice of big love, respect and gratitude.

Thanks guys. Keep up the great work.

26 - World Cup, Les Gets 2023

Déja vu warning!! There's a strong chance you'll get the feeling that you've read this chapter before, but don't panic, you haven't… It's not a glitch in the matrix, you haven't put your bookmark on the wrong page and you're not having some kind of disturbing brain fart… Well, you might be but not because of me… Well, it might be because of me but… Sod it, never mind!

I couldn't bring myself to just add a bit about the World Champs or the last World Cup, so I added both. In fact, I think it was necessary, possibly even my duty. There are similarities but they're very different and the World Cup in Les Gets last year was such a spectacle that I wrote about it as soon as I woke up the next day and wanted to share it.

Anyway, get settled in, make yourself comfortable and here we go.

Yesterday was in-sane!.. I'm sitting down, with a properly foggy head, to write this. It's the day after the 2023 UCI Downhill World Cup race in Les Gets and it was bonkers!.. Again!

The World Champs last year was a *major* highlight and it seemed like it was going to be nigh-on impossible to beat that in the atmosphere department. However, another amazing spectacle unfolded, imprinting even more iconic moments in Les Gets' illustrious DH archives.

An added bonus this year was the return of the full family unit for spectating duties. The tried and tested race day plan had received unanimous approval from the whole gang and was locked and loaded.

PLAN RECAP: into town – bubble lift – chair lift – Chéry summit – start hut – track walk – last corner, last 10 (or so) riders – storm the finish – mayhem – beers – food – party – walk home – bed – Bootiful!

I wasn't going hungry this year though so we quickly slapped some sarnies together, loaded up backpacks with water and snacks, lathered on the sun cream, picked up one of Thomas's mates and set off for town. We'd be needing the suncream too because the whole week had been wall-to-wall blue skies and sunshine. The track was already powder dust and blown out. Race day was going to be a hot, sticky, dusty one.

We'd also lucked out this year because a good friend of ours had lent us a "bipper" for a space in one of the private underground car parks in the centre of town. We could drive down and ditch the van with no need to search for a space and no worries.

The timings for the plan had required a little tweak from last year because the UCI had decided to have a bit of a shake-up and had added semi-finals for the 2023 races.

As a fan, I'm not a fan… The semis convolute the race week in my opinion, add unnecessary risk for the riders and take away from the natural crescendo, one run, winner takes it all nature of DH racing. It just feels like there are two qualifying sessions and at the moment, I hope it disappears as quickly as it arrived.

This change came along with a raft of others resulting from a switch in organisation, coverage and broadcasting partners. Warner Brothers Discovery Sports would be taking over where Red Bull TV left off.

The coverage, user interface and availability left a lot to be desired in my opinion. The stream of frustrated comments online showed that I wasn't alone in thinking so.

The riders, their families, friends, teams, manufacturers, sponsors and hosts graft to deliver an awesome spectacle week in and week out.

The creation and distribution of content is where the results of all that hard work and investment are showcased to the world. It should satisfy the appetite of the loyal fans and it should be used as a tool to attract new ones. It should grow that fan base for the benefit of the whole sport and for all of those dedicated contributors. The raw materials to create spectacular, extensive content are top quality and the coverage and delivery should match that, if not exceed it. I really hope things improve.

Anyway, the inclusion of the semis on race day and the reduced number of riders in the final meant I wasn't quite sure what the timings would be. I didn't want to take any chances, so we set off niiiice and early to avoid traffic, queues and the risk of missing any of the action.

It was perhaps a little too early. The roads were chilled and there were still roadside parking spaces available. We used our fancy-pants, posh parking space nonetheless before walking over to the Mont Chéry bubble. No queue beyond the bottom of the stairs here either… *"We have got the right day haven't we?"*

There was however a decent queue of riders filtering in from the pits or rejoining after finishing a practice run. Thomas started spotting and rattling off names as we climbed the stairs.

We gradually edged up the steps and it turned out that our timing had in fact been perfect… Just as we made it through the turnstiles at the top, the lifties halted all of us civilians to give the riders priority. Nobody's a fan of queuing but on this occasion it was mint.

It was like a front-row position at the barriers of a red-carpet entrance with the stars of the sport filing through. They'd wait and load their bikes right in front of us. Then they'd duck their heads and hop in before the doors slid shut behind them and they were whisked off up the hill.

Jackson Goldstone, Laurie Greenland, Valentina Holt, Greg Minnaar, Nina Hoffman, all filed past. They were all in lovely fresh kit, shiny personalised helmets and delicious bikes, pimped out to the max. We offered the odd quiet word of encouragement "G'won Laurie!"

Thomas already has his sights set on elite-level racing and seeing all these little extra bits just keep adding icing onto his cake of enthusiasm. Izzy was more interested in which ones were the hottest. Haha!

Eventually, some cabins clanked into the station without bike hooks and we were hastily ushered on board by the lifties. The doors slid shut and away we went.

A dude from Paris got squished in with us. He spent a few minutes quietly chuckling to himself at the slightly inappropriate verbal diarrhoea spewing out of Thomas's mouth. We got chatting and he excitedly told us how he'd finished work last night in Paris, jumped in the car with his dad and had driven eight hours straight to Les Gets. It was his first World Cup in the flesh and he was buzzing.

At the top of the lift we bid him farewell and a, "Bonne journée", turned left, appreciated the panorama and mooched over towards the Pointe chairlift. The riders turned right and headed in the other direction towards the two-man Grand Ourse chairlift. That one was reserved for them and would take them up to a warm-up area at the Grand Ourse restaurant, a stone's throw from the start hut and at an elevation of 1746 m.

It was lucky for the riders that they were heading in the opposite direction because our three fired up the vuvuzelas or "f**k-trumpets" as they've been re-branded by Forbike. The wind section was now a year bigger, with stronger lungs and proportionately louder!

Sudden loud noises raise my stress levels and I can be a bad-tempered git for a few minutes before I eventually take a "chill pill" and get on board. It's OK when the action's happening and everybody is getting in among it but when the three lone trumpeters under my "adult" responsibility are scaring the living crap out of dogs, old people, babies, wildlife and people with heart conditions or of a nervous disposition, I'm fired into grumpy-dad-grumble-mode in a nano-second.

Somebody's got to start it though and as they honked our way up the Pointe chair, the call to arms started attracting reciprocal rutting calls from across the mountains. The real deer in the area must have been frantically checking their calendars, spraying deodorant/breath freshener and worrying that they'd got their mating dates mixed up.

We sailed over a fully grown, adult Super Mario (like-ya-do) and arrived at the top station. Same deal as last year: awkward low-level dismount. "Merci" to the lifties, a quick trip to the summit, then the same slip and slide down to the start hut.

Even I was enjoying the noise now. The chairlift was now loaded with people honking and whooping and hollering back at us and we were even making a racket without the f**k-trumpets.

Five-minute countdown for women's semis… 4… 3… 2… 1… And we're off!

We watched the first few women crank out of the start hut, set off through the first few big dusty berms and off the first step down. It doesn't look like much when you see it on TV but standing on the edge of it is another kettle of fish. These girls skip over it without batting an eyelid.

We picked our way across the open meadow, alongside the track and among the blueberry bushes. The crickets in our path dropped their washboards and leaped out of the way as we crunched along.

The next feature of interest is the first flat, fast, long, road gap. It's another one of those things that look like nothing on TV, especially when the riders are travelling at Mach 10 like these guys but when you scramble down the bank and watch them sail past at head height, it's a decent gap and a significant feature.

There was a quick skim through an undulating, dusty section with fine webbed roots for the riders and an ungainly clamber through the undergrowth for us before we arrived at the Les Gets road gap, one of the bigger features on the track.

It had been tamed a little last year with a bigger berm after the landing and the removal of a tree on the outside. This year, the berm had been removed completely and the track now went straight ahead into a larger, more comfortable landing. This would probably be an opportunity for a little, mid-air "breather" for these guys.

We paused again to watch a load of riders sending it, then got back into David Bellamy mode (one for the oldies) and hit the undergrowth.

Some friends of ours had skirted Mont Chéry from Mont Caly to the west to come and meet us. They emerged from the brush and we had a quick catch-up punctuated with whistles, applause, horns, chainsaws and mayhem, as each pilot whizzed by.

We've lived here a while now and these events are excellent social events for the locals. Most people young and old, generational locals and new arrivals like us, turn out for the spectacle. It's really nice bumping into people throughout the day.

It's even better for the kids, especially Izzy, who would periodically be engulfed in a swarm of jabbering teenagers for a couple of minutes before popping out of the other side.

Sketchy 4G granted me just enough packets of data to see where we were up to in the semis, and it was close to the end.

We were just above the lake and Loïc was on track. "Loïc's coming!" I yelled down to Thomas. And when he arrived, he was charging! *"Hellfire!"* He was flying through this section. If he could keep the bike the right way up at this speed, this was going to be quick! *Baphaphaphap(!)* over the roots, whooping the ground as he gapped and pumped the contours to maintain and gain speed, and then *WALLOP!* He was off! He was down!

A massive cloud of dust burst into the air as he hit the deck but he was up and going again straight away. He was

OK but the margins are so tight that that's usually game over as far as a competitive time goes but it ain't over until it's over. It didn't really matter too much anyway, because as one of the top riders his position in the final was protected anyway… What's the actual point?

Well… points actually… There are points on the table in the semis but regardless of that, the biggest personality of this French-hosted weekend could have been injured and out completely on a run that is essentially just an extra practice to him. In addition to that, he now had to get to the bottom, get the bike checked, and get his head together for his final run with a crash fresh in his memory. Not ideal in my opinion.

Loris Vergier came hurtling through second to last and went top, quickly followed by Coulanges who snatched it back off him and made it two for two, having already bagged the fastest qualifying time.

We popped out of the woods onto one of the intersecting fire roads and found some shade to get stuck into our sarnies. Cheese, cucumber and salad cream – my go-to for a high-speed "sanga" fabrication.

Les Gets Ski Club bar had a new location this year so there was no snack bar at the Fanzone by the reservoir. It had been taken over by Red Bull who had already been rinsed of all their freebies. I had been hoping for a cold midpoint beer to wash my sarnies down, but that'd have to wait.

The women's finals were set to start at 1.00 pm, so we finished up our packed lunches and dropped back into the woods for our final descent at more or less the same time.

One by one, the women started coming through. The next section of the track, crisscrosses and blends with some sections of the new elite Ellipse line and our old favourite Dans L'Gaz.

It starts getting much busier and rowdier with spectators from here on down. More people ride the bubble to the mid-station and join those of us descending from the top. Others hike up from the bottom too and can catch the lift back down if they want. More of Thomas's friends appeared and settled into our crew as we descended.

The women finalists kept coming through and to my disappointment, live timings were not available for them on the UCI website. I also couldn't get the footage to stream on the GCN+ app, which I'd begrudgingly subscribed to.

Vali Höll came through and we finally managed to find some info online that filled us in with what was happening. Despite being favourite for the win Vali had crashed in the first set of berms and was out of the running from the get-go.

That meant that Frenchwoman Marine Cabirou who was already sitting in the hot seat, had taken the win. She was followed by Slovenian Monika Hrastnik in 2nd and German Nina Hoffmann in 3rd. The Frenchies would be over the moon.

We were approaching one of my favourite bits of the descent and of the spectating experience, The Black Wood 2.0. I was ready for some slip-n-slide carnage and boss-level beer saves.

We got there though and "*Noooo!*" The crossing to get on the right side of the track no longer existed and no spectators were lining that side of the track either. I could only assume that someone in their "infinite wisdom" had deemed it unsafe. "*Booo!.. But maybe wise...*"

Instead, the path led us away from the track and out into the clearing of the adjacent ski piste. There were a couple of minutes where we couldn't get close to or see one of the best sections of track on the whole course, but luckily, the detour provided some entertainment of its own.

The gradient mirrored that of the track and it was so steep that it was virtually impossible to maintain grip beneath your feet on the grass. When you did lose it, it was steep enough to continue the slide on your backside for quite some distance.

We teetered, slipped and giggled our way down, trying not to scoop up piles of strangers when we did lose it. We dodged others who already had and were sliding down fast from above. We made it to the bottom in one piece and I got my phone out to turn back and film the mayhem.

It's always fun and games until it isn't, and I'd forgotten that my mate was already suffering from a shoulder injury. Rather than me remembering that, like a good friend, and lending him a hand, I was busy filming and laughing. Then I noticed his expression, and it all came flooding back. "Oh sugar! D'you need a hand mate?"

"No, I'm alright cheers, but I did fall on it again and it's *very* sore now."

Turns out he *had* already been carrying a fracture. Slipping down a hill and falling on it probably wasn't the ideal addition to his recuperation. You might be wondering if it was a biking incident that had caused it in the first place. Nope!.. Numpty incident. Slipping on a grassy bank in his own garden. He'd got form.

We paused at the bottom of the Black Wood 2.0 and crossed the track to look back up the track at that tasty section. We could watch the riders speed down through the woods, off the "Flying Scotsman" gap, previously known as "The Swan Dive" gap, previously known as the "Canyon Gap" and off across the piste.

The clock was ticking, and Thomas was getting jumpy. He didn't want to miss the climax at the finish. None of us did. We cracked on, past the "Straight Shooter" jump and walked along the tarmac road that heads out towards the idyllic Pottery in Les Gets. We'd pause and peep over the edge as each rider came through the "Whip Stadium" before cutting down and across the grass.

Another herd of teenagers had appeared and Izzy was absorbed into the blob and disappeared off with some giant human bananas and a human speed camera. We'd be lucky to see her again before the "walk home" phase of the plan.

The universe had answered my earlier request for beer as Nina stumbled across a shiny new can of high-strength "tramp juice" (an umbrella term for any high-strength beer coined by another "Direct Line" mate of mine here in Les Gets) discarded in the grass and cracked it open.

On a normal day, I'd at least have wanted to give it a rinse before going near it, but it's World Cup day! *"Yeah, go on then. I'll have a swig."* We assumed our position at the last corner. Planned and ready for action this time.

We found a spot as close to the track as we could and Thomas said, "I'm just going to try and get to the front with my friends. Is that OK? I'll just see you at the bottom somewhere afterwards."

"Yeah, sure. Stick together, take care and see you in a bit."

The huge meadow slope near the finish section was filling up. More and more people were going with the flow and collecting near the finish area. The atmosphere and energy were flooding down with them and gaining momentum. It was as if the slipstream from every rider whizzing past wound it even further.

The noise had gradually built from those first few f**k-trumpet honks at the start of the day to a crescendoing wall of sound. Chainsaw-body wielders who had been peppered down the side of the mountain had now congealed at the bottom.

Some of them were having chainsaw-offs whirling their motors in giant circles at arm's length. People were screaming, shouting and whooping. Old bike frames and rims had been taking a beating all day long and were still getting the good news, double time.

One guy had what sounded like an actual train horn in a purpose-built backpack. It was a homemade-looking contraption with several horns sticking out of it. Some wires and a circuit box were visible as well as a wire leading to a trigger button in his hand.

Come to think of it, he was probably lucky not to have been taken down by a SWAT team but he'd hit the button and an almighty harmonic blast of sound came from it like an Amtrak train passing a level crossing.

A bright pink blur caught my eye as it flashed through the air. A nearby chainsaw whirler had a huge, pink, rubber dildo stuck to his chainsaw. It was bouncing and dancing around as it got whirled up into the air, around and around.

We'd made it down for more than the top 10 because we'd seen that Bruni was coming down 15th from last and we wanted to be there as part of the atmosphere as he came past.

We could hear him coming and the crowd went bonkers. The dildo-saw was doing double time. Flopping and slapping around like its life depended on it. Bruni soared over the final jump, railed the last berm, pedalled hard, thrust his bike forward over the line and went P1! Over two seconds clear. The crowd went bananas!

After that spill in his semi-final run, Bruni had been the 15th finalist from last and he now had a nervous wait on the hot seat while the next 14 riders came through. Eight more crossed the finish line and Bruni held his spot.

Then it was Andreas Kolb's turn to drop. His considerable frame appeared, sailing through the air over the last jump, locked into the final berm, across the line and fastest.

The French crowd had cheered him on enthusiastically on his way past, but when they saw that he'd knocked Bruni off the top spot, the energy dropped like the tyre pressure from a pinch flat in a rock garden.

Goldstone followed and went 2nd, nudging Bruni down to 3rd.

Brosnan came in next and finished 6th.

Norton crashed on the way down and only managed 30th.

There were only two riders left... Only two Frenchmen left with a chance to seal the deal on home turf. The atmosphere and support for each and every rider had still been top-notch but the anticipation and anxiety in the mob was palpable.

Eventually, Vergier blasted through in the wake of a tidal wave of noise and movement. Over the line and... 2nd.

This was turning into a roller coaster of emotion for the French supporters.

There was just one man left. Benoit Coulanges and he'd been smashing it all week. Fastest qualifier, fastest semi-finalist and if anyone was capable of elbowing their way onto the top step today, it was him. The pressure must have been immense. One opportunity and one run standing between him and glory in front of the home fans.

Not just French home fans either. Living just a few kms down the valley, this was local turf, his summer stomping ground. Destiny was calling too.

He'd been French champ in 2020 and 2021, European silver medallist three times and had even narrowly missed out on a World Championship title in 2021 when he'd finished in 2nd place. He'd been competitive on the circuit since 2017 but was still yet to claim a deserving place on the top step of the world stage.

The cauldron of noise was almost constant now; it was amazing that there was anything left in reserve to achieve the tsunami that roared when Coulanges came through. It was deafening, exhilarating and amazing. Arms in the air, flares, horns, clapping, chainsaws, beer.

The wave of support cascaded down towards us from the sides of the track, out of sight above us. Then he launched into the air and the TV camera on a long pivot arm swung a wide arc to follow him. He blazed into the last corner and pedalled frantically for the line.

He stretched across it with every ounce of effort and the screen went green. He was up! He was fastest! He'd only gone and bleedin' won it!

Almost instantaneously, a cloud of dust launched into the air. It looked like a sandstorm rolling off the desert. It took a second to mentally compute that it had been being thrown up from the herd of fans bolting out of the blocks and forwards towards the finish line. As soon as it did, I followed suit.

I darted forward following the path that Thomas would have taken in front of us. I started to trot for a few metres then realised I'd hadn't checked everyone else was still with me. I turned to look for Nina first who was in close pursuit. No sign of John and his knackered shoulder. He'd probably decided that staying put was a sensible move. "*Oops. Sorry again, mate.*"

Too late. Keep moving. Go with the flow. Nina and I stuck together and joined the surge, marching down the track.

The spectacle at the bottom was insane! Coulanges had slung his bike and was immediately mobbed by a stream of friends and fans. More Gendarmes were on hand after previous years' carnage and they attempted to bundle Benoit behind the barriers and toward the interview area. He was so elated that he was still fighting to get back and jump around with the fans.

He continued celebrating behind the barriers, among the cameras with fellow riders and team staff, and across the barriers with supporters.

We found out later that Izzy had been close to the lead pack and had legged it down the finish straight in hot pursuit of the bananas and speed camera. Thomas and his mates weren't far behind.

I know this might sound a little bit like maverick parenting and maybe it is, but what an experience. Our kids and the others round here have quite a bit of experience with things like this though. Maybe not quite on this scale but there are regularly large events attended by thousands and the local kids stick together and look out for each other. The crowds and village are always laced with familiar faces who'll keep an eye out for each other.

Benoit was eventually ushered to an interview area. He had a short interview that looked like two people awkwardly shouting into each other's ears in a club but not really hearing anything. He kept pausing to look at the scene, communicate his appreciation to the crowd and whip it up even more!

He was going to make the absolute most of this and as soon as the interview was over he scaled the barriers, dived back into the mêlée and was hoisted aloft. For the next few minutes he surfed around the finish area while the wall of noise continued. A big, beautiful wall of noise.

A "police siren" had joined the din, as had a bloke with a megaphone who was now conducting the thousands-strong choir with chants of "Boah-poah-loah-poah-poah-loah-poah" to the tune of The White Stripes – Seven Nation Army followed by repeat renditions of the French National Anthem, La Marseillaise.

Coulanges was joined above the sea of heads and hands by a disco of flares, flags, posters banners, horns and signs including the ever-growing range of Bruni parodies. We were just a few layers of bodies in front of Smurf Bruni.

Watching someone ring every last drop out of a peak life experience and a monumental achievement was an absolute pleasure to behold, especially someone who had worked so hard for so long and come so close *so* many times. Doing it surrounded by people who were totally behind him and knew what it meant was even more special.

We stood, watched and took it all in. The crowd worked in some kind of psychic harmony to deliver Coulanges to the podium, ready for the presentations.

The ladies came out first, relishing the atmosphere and the crowd went nuts as Marine took to the top step and received her trophy. She looked over the moon.

The men came out to more of the same and Coulanges received his trophy amid more passionate renditions of La Marseillaise. It looked like he never wanted this to end, understandably, but he knew it had to and was making sure to enjoy every sensation and imprint as much of it on his memory as possible.

There were more podiums for the teams and the series leaders where Bruni and the French crowd got to spend some quality time and mutual appreciation. As the crowd began to disperse we checked in with the kids and decamped to the Les Gets Vélo Club bar once again to get a drink and regroup.

Phew! That was intense... Again!

We hung out around town and the pits, bumped into friends, had a couple more drinks and a pulled pork burger. We checked out the party at the Commencal tent and in the party hub in the centre of town then had a magical starlit walk home.

What a freakin' day! An amazing spectacle to have been a part of once again and a fairytale story, climaxing in glorious mayhem.

27 - Top Dogs

The World Cup racers are just one branch of riders at the top of the tree and I really want to give a special shout out to them and the top dogs of the sport in *every* discipline. These guys and girls perform some mind-meltingly awesome feats of riding, for our entertainment, enjoyment and inspiration.

When this lot push their limits, they're pushing the limits of the whole sport. They are building on a lifetime of personal progression, standing on the shoulders of giants who came before. They are laying extensions to that conveyor belt of progress and we're all tucked in behind, steadily cranking our way forward.

The following is just a "wee snifter" to take the edge off. It's a nod to the disciplines and the athletes and the cycles of change. There's a deep, deep rabbit hole of talent and inspiration, so this is just a scratch of the surface for a sniff of the whiff.

—

25 years deep at the top of the game,
GOAT is the title and Minnaar's the name.

Bagging the trophies and heir to that title,
Bruni is super and his presence is vital.

His high-speed control is a joy to behold,
6 Champs, 4 Cups (overall) and just 29 years old.

Goldstone continues his prodigal rise,
with a visit to Wales for the Hardline prize.

He moved up to elite and showed no fear,
claiming 2 World Cup wins, in a competitive year.

On GB soil it was local, World Champs glory.
Charlie Hatton, Fort Bill, a dream media story.

Höll's campaign was a dominant crusade.
You get the sense that history's being made.

Hoffman and Cabirou were left in her wake,
but the rest of those girls want a slice of that cake.

In the pedalling world, Schurter is king among kings.
His career, like his whips, have certainly got wings.

FOR THE LOVE OF MOUNTAIN BIKING

9 Cup overalls and 10 Champs in the bag.
So laden with medals his shoulders should sag.

Pidcock continues to morph between genres,
from tarmac to dirt and more XC honours.

Puck Pieterse decisively burst on the scene.
Twin titles in the bag, from debutant to Queen.

This could signal a changing of the guard,
but the likes of Keller and Ferrand-Prévot, will be fighting
back hard.

In the enduro game, the magic, was indeed number 3.
Triple titles for Rude and Courdurier, make for a heck of a
spree.

At Rampage, Bienvenido flipped the massive canyon gap.
A run that bagged awards, and would be difficult to cap.

It was Brendog's run that dished helpings of gnar.
Elevated heart-rate from viewing, the most uncomfortable
by far.

This year though saw the resurgence of a vet.
Cam Zink bagged the win, with a massive "backed" down-
step.

The absence of the women was somewhat of a shame.
Their uptake in MTB, could practically double the whole
game.

In 23 for Hardline, Welsh wind and rain stopped play,
and for the first time in history, the gang took a long-haul
trip away.

Destination Tassie for the riders pressing send.
A few enormous spills but thankfully all are on the mend.

Dunne pipped king Kerr to wrestle the top spot from his
grasp,
but it was Gracey Hemstreet's historic run that made the
bike world gasp.

Johansson brings an abundance, of style to our slopes.
Triple, triple-crown supremacy, actualising all of his hopes.

Velez, Slavik and the boys have been ripping up the street,
drawing gasps from burgeoning crowds, in the South
American heat.

When we're searching for entertainment and our inspiration
needs,
we need look no further than our YouTube and Insta feeds.

Here we find more top-dogs, kindred spirits of our creed,
creating content for our pleasure, and taking up the lead.

Alvo, Pilgrim, Wibmer, Hills, MacAskill and Semenuk too,
bringing creativity, personality and showing what it's possible
to do.

There are many Yodas out there, that none of us might
know.
Bike masters in anonymity, shredding away from the
limelight's glow.

There are absent faves without a doubt,
so no offence, if I've missed some out.

An internal doff of the cap, all the same
and my thanks for all your work, at the top of our beautiful
game.

–

Most of the top dudes look like they are having a blast and why wouldn't they be. Yeah, there's undoubtedly a lot of hard-work, dedication, sacrifice and a considerable element of risk but it's still those same souls enjoying that same joyful pleasure of riding bikes.

We can all relate to that and they can relate to us. There's that connection and understanding from our shared experience of just riding mountain bikes. Same sensations, same progression, same experiences, same trails (within reason!) and same terrain.

It's been a privilege to witness so many of the top riders at close quarters over the last few years, performing at the top of their games.

It always astonishes me how accessible everything is and how approachable they all are. The whole village transforms into giant pits and it's awesome mooching around and having a proper nosey into the elite-level world.

So many of these guys make time for the fans and especially the little dudes, mine included. It really does make the kids feel amazing, and inspired, so full credit for making the effort.

That camaraderie I've mentioned carries right to the top. There seems to be a cooperation amongst competitors that you don't always see in a lot of other sports and I think it speaks volumes for the nature and culture of ours.

There's that connection of shared experience, an understanding of the mutual risk and consequences that add an element of grace to the competitive beast.

The riders support and encourage each other. They are aware that there are so many other factors that can play a hand in the fate of their run, week or even season. They are all facing the terrain, the tracks, the features, the weather, mechanical luck and themselves as much as they are facing each other. When someone is victorious, so many of their peers seem so genuinely pleased for them.

At the end of the day though, they are all still big kids playing out on bikes.

I was at a charity fundraiser burlesque night a few years ago with a couple of non-riding mates and we ended up seated at a table with a number of World Cup riders.

My mates had no idea who these guys were and merrily chatted away getting to know them. Afterwards, they said they were blown away by what good natured and humble vibes they'd all given off. They also concluded that that seemed to go hand in hand with a lifestyle of travelling and hanging out with your friends riding bikes that suddenly seemed very appealing to them, even as non-riders!

Now don't get me wrong. I'm not so naive as to think that it's all sweetness and light. I know I'm on the outside looking in and I'm sure there'll be some clashes, rivalries, beefs, history and politics but on the whole, the vibe just feels pretty sweet.

Interestingly, living around here, you get the inside scoop from time-to-time. The teams and riders rent local accommodation, eat in the restaurants, shop in the shops and party in the bars, when it's time to celebrate. The grapevine inevitably does its thing. There's the odd tale of someone getting above their station, but on the whole, the feedback matches my own experience, that the vast majority are decent dudes, leaving positive impressions. Some of them are *top-class, high-quality* individuals.

So thanks guys for blazing the trail. Thanks for your hard work and dedication. Thank you for the inspiration and the entertainment. Keep up the great work!

28 - Young Blood

The top dogs are doing a great job holding the torch at the cutting edge of the sport, but the young dudes are blazing a trail and are hot on their heels.

These new generations are benefitting from the abundance of content and inspiration that they are exposed to, both from the big guns and from their peers.

They are easily able to see what's being done, what's possible and how to do it. Throw in access to better coaching, information, technique and inspiration, and the results are spectacular!

They are starting younger and riding harder, from the little ones up to the juniors. As they continue to grow in size, strength, skill and experience, they're going to become formidable.

I'm sure this is being reflected all over the world but the standard of the young guns around here is phenomenal.

One example that sticks with me is going riding with Thomas a couple of years ago. He was 11 and we met a mate of his who was 14 or 15 at the time. We met him at the top of the Chavannes Express, exchanged pleasantries and dropped into L'Arpette, a blue in Les Gets starting at the top of the Chavannes lift.

The two of them were on *"full send"* immediately! Charging hard and schralping the living daylights out of every berm in sight. After the first windy section, there's a bank of four table tops running alongside a 4x4 access track. T's mate proceeded to suicide no-hander each one back-to-back without a care in the world. *"Oooookkkaaayyy. I'll just hang out here at the back boys."*

I wanted to include an exact quote here but I can't find the footage so I'll have to give you the gist instead.

The World Championships were held in Glasgow, Scotland in 2023 and after the downhill finals, the camera cut back to Clare Balding. She looked visibly taken aback by what she had just witnessed and said something along the lines of:

"Well, I don't think I can remember spending an hour watching something and being *so* on the edge of my seat the whole time."

For a top, long-time sports presenter to look, and sound, so flabbergasted, speaks volumes about the spectacle of DH MTB and its potential with a much wider audience.

She also said, *"I can just hear kids up and down the country saying, 'I want to do that' and their parents saying, 'No way!'"*

Haha! I totally get that. I got mine into it when they were little and it was just with the intention of sharing something I loved to do. I loved it and I hoped to enjoy doing it with them.

Izzy wasn't fussed but Thomas loved it. Progressing and spending time, doing something we both love has been an absolute joy. As the tables begin to turn though and as he begins to exceed my capabilities, it has become a bit more nerve-wracking.

I've had a few, "Errrm. What have I unleashed?" moments, like when he went out last summer with his mates and returned to tell me that he'd ticked off almost all the features on the Elite level "Ellipse" line in Les Gets... Despite the risks, the huge list of benefits I've listed in this book massively offset the concern. Those and the fact he and his mates absolutely love it.

Also, their judgement is probably better than mine now. They aren't reckless. They've followed the conveyor belt of progress. They assess and calculate and they aren't afraid to stand down if they're not feeling it. They know that every day is different and next time that same thing might be a synch. They are collaborative and supportive and want to take positive, progressive steps forward, not backwards.

Another great by-product as a dad is I'm having the great pleasure of enjoying it all over again from a kid's perspective. I get to ride with a new set of little buddies who will pull me along, challenge me and teach me new stuff. I'm tucked in the slip-stream and hanging on for the time being but I know it won't be long before they're just too far ahead and I'll be lost in the wake.

It's a real pleasure to watch these new generations of young riders embarking on their lifelong mountain bike love affairs. It's so exciting to watch the new waves of talent keep pulsing through, knowing the fun they'll have, the skills they'll build, the good times they'll enjoy, the progression they'll push and the creativity they'll unleash.

29 - Champéry

The summer-season operations usually come to an end in mid-September on the French side of the Portes du Soleil, but it's become an end-of-season tradition to have a visit or two to the Swiss side of the border... A few last, local-ish, lift-assisted "hurrahs" to wring the last drips of juice out of the summer.

As the last bum-shaped mud impressions get jet-washed off the lift seats in Les Gets, Morzine, Avoriaz and Châtel, those of us looking for an extra fix of uplift don't have to look too far.

On the other side of the border in the Région Dents Du Midi, the Swiss eek things out for a little while longer. Quite a lot longer actually, and it's well worth making the drive up and over the Col du Corbier from Le Biot, through Abondance and Châtel and around "the back" for some bonus weekend lift-assisted downhill action.

In 2023, Morgins bike park was closed while its ageing chairlift was being replaced with a snazzy new télécabine. Morgins is a great deal of fun and was well missed as a riding option. We're all really looking forward to getting back out there again this year.

The other destination to head for is Champéry/Les Crosets which always holds out late and which was still open for bike passengers until 29th October in 2022. We've been there and ridden bikes late on in previous years then gone back just a few short weeks later to ski and snowboard.

End-of-season Swiss missions have always been with mates in the past but a lot of mine were out of action or unavailable this year, for one reason or another. This time, it was Thomas driving the charge, "Can we go and ride in Champéry next weekend, Dad?"

No sooner had I said "Heck yeah!" than he was messaging his mates to see who else could come.

Now then… Do you remember that one-handed wheelie I mentioned earlier? The one way back in the day at the start of the book? It was the one that I tried, nailed it and impressed Thomas?.. Well, that was part of a fairly intense wheelie and manual sesh up the road behind our house. It was also during the final week that the local lifts were open and I'd been out riding whenever I got the chance. I'd been trying new stuff, pushing hard and trying to squeeze in as much progress as possible. All that effort and activity had resulted in a tweak in my lower back.

I hadn't listened to the warning signs… It had felt tight after all that yanking on the bars and balancing… It hadn't felt happy with all the extra hucking around the bike park but I'd been having fun and I kept pushing it. Then, it had had enough, and it bit back, going into a painful spasm.

Then, I didn't listen again… I was really excited about Champéry and I wanted to be in good condition for it, so I kept training. I kept trying to stretch, I kept doing some small steady pedally rides to try and loosen it up and when they made it worse, I walked instead.

Everything was making it worse though. Every bit of bodily feedback was saying *"REST IT!"* But my monkey mind was saying, *"Maybe something else will work and the next thing, and the next thing, and the next thing."*

When the weekend rolled around, I could barely get out of bed. I hadn't been sleeping well because of it and I wasn't even sure I was going to be able to drive the van to take the boys. I'd looked into physios and "chiros" but it had been too late to get an appointment.

We pushed our plans from Saturday to Sunday in the hope that the extra day would buy me a bit more time to recover and I spent some time prepping. I did my bike as well just in case. I was still holding out hope that some miracle might cause something to click into place and release all that tension and pain. I gingerly packed the van ready for an early start the next morning.

We woke the next morning and I figured I'd at least be able to drive the boys over there and be on hand if they needed anything. It was freakin' freezing too. We'd been used to temperatures nearer to the 30 mark and all of a sudden it had dipped to 4°C. I remembered that I'd felt particularly cold in Champéry in the past, so I stuck a bunch of extra layers in and a sleeping bag, just in case I found myself sitting waiting in the van for hours.

One of Thomas's riding mates, who's a few years older than him, had answered the rallying call and we set off to pick him up.

Like any self-respecting teenager, Nino met us in a T-shirt... I asked him in French if he'd be warm enough and told him that I had spares if he was cold at any point in the day. He poo-paahed that and said he'd be fine. He said he'd probably be too hot when he started riding and the sun got higher.

We followed the route of the river Dranse, winding down the valley from Morzine towards Thonon-les-Bains. We hung a right beneath the buttress of rock that hovers about the entrance to Le Biot and skirted up the side of the cliffs and on to the Col de Corbier. We wound and weaved down the other side and into the Vallée D'Abondance.

It's a lovely drive down this valley from Abondance and on to Châtel. In contrast to the tighter rugged edges of the part of the Dranse valley we'd just hopped over from, this one feels spacious and open. There are beautiful views of magnificent peaks. It's got an old wild west feel to it as though settlers would have explored up and over the cols and found a fertile, sheltered open valley to set up camp, raise their cows and make cheese. I'm sure this mental image contains some glaring historical and cultural errors but that's always what it feels like in my head.

From Châtel, the road winds up across a lower col, and over the Swiss border into Morgins. We wound down through Morgins and past the big concrete structure of the new télécabine lift station.

Just beyond the town boundary, we turned off right for a windy short-cut through to the road from Monthey. Monthey is in the Rhône valley bottom a few kilometres from the eastern end of Lake Geneva in Switzerland. The road snakes up, into the Illiez valley, terminating at Champéry at the top.

An hour and a half after leaving home, we pulled into the big car park opposite the imposing Champéry cable car station. Several thousand tonnes of concrete-housing anchor monstrous spindles. Giant lift cables haul two cars, as big and red as London buses up and down to the Croix de Culet peak 900 m elevation above.

Driving was never going to help my back and I nervously lowered myself out of the van and gradually creaked into an upright position. It was freezing, and despite looking like he was frozen, I still couldn't interest Nino in an extra layer. I walked around the car park to try and loosen things up. Everything was going to be softly-softly today.

The lads already went out riding together on their own but the World Cup track in Champéry is a tasty ribbon of gnar and if they ended up riding that, I'd prefer to be hovering around, on hand, just in case.

Bite-sized steps of progress was my plan for the day.

Step 1 was to drive to Champéry, which had been a success.

Step 2 was to have a gentle stretch and see how everything felt. If it felt OK, I'd stick my bike in the cable car, go up with the lads and see how things went. If not, I'd sack the bike off, go up in the lift on foot, then ride it back down and meet them at the bottom.

It felt "OK" after the stretches, so we kitted up, pedalled across the road, round the back of the lift station, in through the sliding doors, beeped through the turnstiles and boarded the lift.

These late season lift openings are a limited service. The lift only runs every 30 minutes, so we had to wait a few minutes before the operator hopped on board. He slid the doors closed, crackled some communications on his radio and hit the "go" button.

By the time he did, there were maybe 20 bikes and bikers on board and a bunch of hikers. We set sail up and over the town and the terrain below steepened as we rose.

The cable rises up the western face from the valley and glaring down at us from the eastern side are our old mates the Dents du Midi – that breathtakingly formidable range of serrated peaks topping out with Haute Cime on the right-hand end, at an impressive 3257m.

Autumn hadn't quite taken hold yet and the green meadows that fringed the valley bottom gave way to the exposed grey bedrock and scree of the Dents. The overnight precipitation had sieved a dusting of icing sugar snow over the tops of the whole range, adding a finishing flourish to our spectacular view.

The driver hit the button for the doors at the top and we weaved out of the lift station, plopping out onto the stoney clearing. I still had significantly limited mobility but I figured I'd got enough to give it a go.

"Giving it a go" was baby step number 3. If it was too much, I'd abort and find the easiest way back to the van, whether that was by road, track, walking or getting back to the cable car and riding that back down.

At this time of year there are a reduced number of trails open in this area because access via the Swiss Mossettes chairlift is no longer possible. You *can* pedal up and ride them if you wish but there's still plenty of lift-accessed trails to go at and what it lacks in quantity, it makes up for in quality.

From the top of the télécabine there are two options. The first is to roll down the track a short way and pedal up to a small summit at the top of the Crosets chairlift. There's a brilliant red trail that runs down alongside it. It's the same "super-fun red downhill section" that we rode as part of the Pass'Portes du Soleil. It's a beauty. It's tight, fast and flowy and has that real roller-coaster feel.

At the end of it you can jump back on the Crosets chairlift and head back up top for another go, or roll down the road through Les Crosets village and pick up another red called Sundance.

Sundance is a fun single-track/freeride style section followed by a flowy compacted gravelly jump line that runs alongside a stream bed. Then it's back out onto a shingle fire road, followed by a tarmac road with stunning views all the way back down to town and the base of the cable car.

The second option from the top of the cable car is to hang-a-left and get straight into the red Chevreuil trail. From this you can branch off onto the black World Cup track Coupe de Monde.

The black Coupe de Monde option is a handful. Properly tasty. Steep, rocky and requiring total engagement top-to-bottom. It's slightly different now but was the scene of that infamous World Championship winning run in the wet by Danny Hart in 2011. In the most challenging, sopping-wet conditions, he went almost 12 seconds faster than anyone else!

The spectacle was so impressive that it prompted Rob Warner to scream that infamous line "How does Danny Hart sit down with balls that big!"

Well, having ridden this track a few times in the past, and at a fraction of that speed, I can attest that it is a handful. It's a track where I feel like I'm just constantly trying to reign things in, to stop things getting away from me. There is no room to relax – anywhere – and any complacency or loss of concentration can result in things getting very out of hand, very quickly… It's great fun though.

I remember thinking that if you're ever feeling a bit lethargic, just go for a lap at Champéry and that'll wake you up in no time! That track is like the MTB trail version of smelling salts.

Despite the ground being wet, Nino was all for dropping straight in at the deep end and going for it.

I suggested a run over at the red to get them warmed up first and to let me see how much I could manage. There were no arguments from the lads and off we went.

The Crosets red was a good option for Step 3. It was easy to get out of if I needed to and I could make my way down the grassy expanse of the neighbouring "ski piste" if I was struggling.

The lads set off at Mach 10! I cautiously dropped in behind and was met with something else I hadn't factored into the equation... *Frost*! A good proportion of the dirt on the track was frozen solid and slippy as heck. Just what I needed!

Some had frozen but the top few millimetres had started to thaw making for a greasy layer on top of a frozen base. Some sections were not frozen but slick and wet and some had been sheltered from the rain by trees and were still fairly dry and dusty. Oh yes!.. Nice and testing!

This was going to be challenging, Especially given how rigid I was on the bike. I could already hear the boys squealing and cheering as they got loose ahead of me. They were immediately slipping, sliding and speeding their way down the trail.

They now belong to a whole generation of "schralpaholics" and the evidence was drawn in the dirt in front of me as I picked my way down. What I was seeing as a challenge, they were seeing as extra-bonus good-times. Awesome!

I couldn't jump and I couldn't move around effectively above the bike to maintain optimal grip but I was *out!* I was riding my bike and I was in the mountains. I was riding Champéry with my boy and his buddy, and with a big grin/grimace from ear-to-ear.

I made it down the red and we decided that we'd continue and complete a full top-to-bottom run. We rolled past the lift, across the car park and down the smooth tarmac through Les Crosets.

We found the sign at the entrance to Sundance on the right-hand-side of the road and dropped in again. Nino led the way with Thomas close behind and me bringing up the rear. The boys were off again and I was following along doing the mountain bike equivalent of tip-toeing.

This section is classic, red single-track with some steep switchbacks, rocks sections and roots. It pops out into a stream valley and crosses a bridge where the character of the trail changes completely. The next section has been rebuilt in the last few years and is more of a straighter flow trail with a whole bunch of fun jumps and gap options.

Then it's a fire road followed by tarmac back to town. I'm not really interested in road biking but I do love a nice smooth, fast section of tarmac descent from time-to-time. Even better when you can overtake the odd car. Hehe!

We pulled up back at the cable car station and my back was definitely loosening up. Step 4 was to keep going and keep taking it steady.

We loaded back on the lift for Round 2 and it was much busier this time. We were jam-packed like sardines and there were bikes stacked on top of bikes by the time the lifty hit the "go button".

This time when we rolled out of the top of the lift station, we swung left and headed for Chevreuil and Coupe De Monde. These tracks are split into sections, each punctuated by an intersection with a 4x4 track/fire-road. Chevreuil has four sections and Coupe de Monde five. The tracks are one and the same for the first three sections.

The first section departs from the side of the cable car station and blasts through woodland before popping out of the trees into high alpine meadow and joining the first track cutting through a hamlet of chalets.

At the next switchback the bike trail drops back into the woodland and tracks through some winding bermed corners and a couple of sketchy root drops.

It's then out onto a second 4x4 track, between a couple of chalets and more or less straight ahead before immediately stepping down, back into the woods for the 3rd section.

After a couple of steep rocky berms the trail straightens out and speeds up, clattering over roots and dialling up the level of focus. It also starts feeling exposed with sections of netting on the left-hand side and what feels like a steep and considerable drop if you were to go over and miss a net. *"Eyes on the trail Jimbo. Don't think about it."*

I wasn't even thinking about my back now either. Adrenaline was flowing, total focus and self-preservation had taken over.

The trail tightened into a few more tight, steep, stepped berms in the trees before opening up again. We soon popped out onto the 3rd 4x4 track intersection beside a ski chairlift station.

"Phew! You have our attention!"

The track splits here, Right for red Chevreuil and double-back left on yourself for the black Coupe de Monde. This is the official start point for that 2011 World Championship track.

We stuck to the red for this run, turning right and pedalling a little way along the 4x4 track before dropping in to the left again and away we went!

A little traverse across the grass meadow lulls you into a false sense of security, and then it gets rowdy real quick as the trail turns downhill into the trees. The gradient increases and so does the gnar! It's flowy but it's steep, it's fast with a few rocks, a few roots and a few "whoops!"

Back out on the road once again and that's it for Chevreuil.

It was a roll down the single-lane road back to Champéry for me but at the next switchback of the road another 4x4 track continues straight on into the woods and meets another intersection with "Coupe de Monde". The boys decided they'd ride that section but I was doing way better than expected and didn't want to risk taking a step backwards at this stage in the game.

I waved them off and set off down the road. A few minutes later I was back at the van and so were they, looking a little more wild and wide-eyed than the last time I'd seen them.

"How was that?" I asked. "Genial!" (Awesome in French) and "Sick!" came the replies.

I started farting about with some kit and Thomas asked how my back was, "D'you know what?" I said, "I think it feels better than it has all week."

"Mountain biking solves everything," Nino said in French… Yep! Such wisdom from one so young.

They were buzzing but we decided it was time for a bite to eat so we whacked the bikes in the van and headed off in search of human fuel.

It was toasty warm now. Nino's T-shirt came into its own as we sat in the sun at the restaurant next to the lift station and ate some banging pizzas. Refuelled and rehydrated, we saddled up for the afternoon's action!

We squished back on the lift, rolled out at the top and headed straight for some more laps of the Crosets red to warm up, then picked up Sundance back to the bottom of the cable car. I was feeling better and better as the day went on. I was starting to send it a bit harder and was soon clearing most of the jumps and making the landings. *"This was goooood!"*

Once back at the top, we went back down Chevreuil/ Coupe De Monde and the boys dipped off for the whole of the black this time while I skipped it, finished Chevreuil and met them back at the bottom.

We'd got into a real flow now but the day was drawing to a close and we were starting to tire. It was time to start thinking about heading home.

We hit up Chevreuil again for the last run of the day and I decided that I couldn't come all the way to Champéry and not at least ride some of the black. We went straight onto the 4x4 track at the next hairpin in the road and headed for the final section of Coupe de Monde.

I was still debating chickening out, right until I dropped in.

The gnar dial clicked up to 11 immediately. There's a steep rocky right-hander and a series of "big" steps where I was literally nothing more than a passenger, holding on for dear life! Thankfully everything stayed upright. I got down without any incidents and I even managed to enjoy it.

Don't get me wrong… It had been a flipping handful. My riding had not been a pretty sight by any stretch of the imagination but my back had held up and by the time I popped out at the bottom I was fizzing with excitement and over the moon.

The boys were buzzing too. Buzzing from the whole day and that's really what it had all been about. I wouldn't have been bothered if I hadn't ridden at all but being able to spend most of the day riding with them had been a mega bonus.

I was looking forward to coming back for another round when I was fighting fit but for now we packed up and "got the hell out of 'Dodge'".

I dropped the lads off for a "secret freeride" on the way home just to really knacker them out before picking them up at the bottom and dropping Nino back home.

All that tension and spasm I'd gradually melted out of back during the day was cryogenically frozen back into place on the drive back. When we finally got home, I had to extract myself from the van at glacial speed. I was really paying the price now but it had been worth it. Now that we'd ticked this big day trip off, I could give it a rest and let my back recover in peace.

Things improved significantly over the next few days. It almost felt as though the riding had contributed an overall improvement… I'd like to say mountain biking does indeed solve everything but to be fair it also helped cause the problem in the first place. Haha!

Anyway… What a day… What *another* day!

Thanks for having us Région Dents Du Midi… Already looking forward to the next time.

30 - Creativity, Art and Style

We humans are creative beings. Our ability to imagine, visualise and deliver our ideas is what has set us apart from the other animals and accelerated our evolution as a species.

Art is the application of that imagination and creativity, combined with skill, to produce something beautiful or something which stimulates emotions, thoughts, ideas and beliefs.

Style is that distinctive presentation, an element of individuality which can imbibe something with even more appealing characteristics. It adds personality and identity to that artistic expression.

I've repeatedly mentioned creativity and style throughout this book. There's creativity and artistry laced through the trails, the features, the bikes, the clothes, the shoes, the helmets and the kit, but for me it's the riding itself where the creativity really shines.

There's obviously the speed and the risk and the drama. There are the thrills, the spills and the rush, but mountain biking is an activity awash with creativity, artistry, imagination and style.

There are infinite ways to ride the same terrain. There are endless interpretations with differing line choices, speed, tricks, tweaks and personal flair. All of them add individual expression and a unique air.

We're being creative in so many aspects of our riding and we're adding our individual style and interpretation to the things we ride.

The result… is *Art*.

When we think of art, we usually think of music, paintings, sculptures, movies, writing and dance.

But riding is poetry in motion. It's an exquisite dance with the terrain, the environment and gravity. There's a rhythm, fluidity and flow, tracing brush strokes on the canvas of 3D reality.

It can be planned and rehearsed, refined and polished. A line can be ridden with absolute intent, placing the bike in specific spots at specific times. The right jump and the right trick at the right time for maximum steeze. Filling in the transitions with tweaks, touches and detail. Creating and building a symphony of motion and expression.

It's even present when it's add-lib. Some is more akin to improvised jazz, with riders interpreting and reacting in the moment to create a line that works. And when it works, it feels amazing and it looks magnificent.

Most often our art is created for fleeting moments in time and space before they're suddenly gone. They might not be witnessed by anyone, simply created and vanishing. That doesn't mean it didn't exist though and it doesn't mean it wasn't beautiful. Sometimes they're witnessed by a handful of others and sometimes they are captured and recorded to be enjoyed by millions and shared again and again.

That art is extended, enhanced and encapsulated by the craft and talent of the filmmakers and producers. They create the choreography and cinematography which strikes a chord and ignites our emotions.

Masters of the sport use gravity's engine to trace magnificent trails of movement across the ground and through the air, pushing the boundaries of possibility in pursuit of artistic creation. It is a pleasure to witness and a joy to behold.

So, mountain biking is not just a sport, not just a culture, not just a form of exercise. It's art! And we, my friends, are artists.

31 - God Mode

Some days you're riding sub-par, some days you ride like a steaming pile of dog turds and some days, your bike chows-down on your scrotum! Most days though, you ride pretty damn well, but some days… Some days, you ride like a God!

You know the days I'm talking about. I'm sure some fine, rose-tinted memories have probably just flooded back into your mind. Stand out moments where it all came together. You could do no wrong. Your mind, body and reactions were all on point.

You were riding fast and confident. You could tick off tricks and features that you'd never even dared to attempt before, and they weren't just achieved, you annihilated them! You were just faster, stronger, sharper and cleaner. You were riding with maximum steeze.

Those are special days when you wish there was a drone and film crew following to capture the action. Damn! It feels so good, it feels like it deserves it.

Some days, even your mates notice. "Man, you're on it today pal!"

You are just "in-the-zone". Accelerating away, making distance, jumping further, whipping bigger, hitting the sweet spot on every landing, hooking into the perfect lines in every turn with pinpoint accuracy. You're braking at the last minute but still rolling off them at exactly the right moment to carry maximum speed through and out of every corner.

You feel like you are gliding over the rough stuff, dancing through the technical. You can lock into manuals every time and carry speed without the slightest effort. You're reading the trail quicker, looking further ahead and it feels terrific!

Some days, it's not just you though. Some days it's a collective experience. Some kind of mass, God-mode state has been engaged and you *and* your riding buddies have elevated in synchronicity.

These days are some of my favourites… You're like a squadron of fighter jets, swooping, soaring, rolling, barrelling and speeding down the mountain and through the woods.

You're a rhythmic blur of speed and style, totally in tune, charging and sending, ebbing and flowing. You are playing with the limits of close-quarter manoeuvres as a single cohesive entity, like a murmur of starlings. You are riding tight, anticipating each other's lines and intentions with almost instantaneous, telepathic abilities.

You can spread out. Peeling left! Peeling right! Hitting different lines and features, crossing each other's paths and converging back together, falling into line when the trails tighten before spreading again.

You all know that you're all on it and it's a seriously special feeling.

Whether it's the symphony of collective flow or one of those days where you alone have ascended to another plane of riding ability, those days should be cherished in the memory. Those days are gold dust! They are the peak moments and absolutely priceless.

32 - Finish Line

Well!.. I think I've pretty much summed it up... Surely it's pretty difficult to argue against mountain biking being, indisputably, awesome!

Without taking anything else into account, riding your bike simply brings joy... Simple... Nuff said... Game over.

On top of that though, doing it builds strength, fitness and skill. It engages focus and concentration, improving judgement and reactions.

We become self-motivated, supportive team-players who get to share peak experiences hanging out with our mates.

We're project managers, builders and mechanics. We're amateur meteorologists, geologists and first responders.

We're independent and collaborative. We explore, adventure and travel. We're creative, imaginative, visionary and artistic.

So many of mountain biking's attributes, incidentals and byproducts are proven contributors to human health, happiness and well-being.

The sport draws us into nature where our appreciation of its characteristics, patterns and rhythms grows. The more we know it, the more we love it and the more we love it, the more we cherish it.

The top guys are living the dream, having a blast, pushing the boundaries and inspiring us all. The young guns are coming on strong, taking things to the next level, learning valuable lessons in resilience, determination, planning and preparation.

Heck. Never mind Duke of Edinburgh Awards. Just slap "mountain biker" on a CV and you should be good to go!

Surely it's a big ol' green flag for any employer or investor.

Althoooouuuugh… We should probably admit to a couple of potential, minor weaknesses.

If you do employ a mountain biker, there is the possibility of a loss of focus and a vacant stare from time-to-time.

This is nothing to worry about, simply a case of *"Doo it, doo it"* doing the rounds. I'd highly recommend prescribing an afternoon off, to go for a ride and get it out of their system. Efficiency and effectiveness will improve exponentially as a result.

The second drawback might be lengthy toilet breaks. These are most likely the result of getting sidetracked by "bikeporn" while having a poo. Wi-fi jammers in the loos are a tad excessive so I'd just let this one slide. Maybe give a little to get a little here. They'll be much happier when they re-emerge and therefore more productive.

Joking apart, the last year or so has been a challenging time for the mountain bike industry. Covid upset the apple cart, the supply chains and the normal patterns of the market. Other factors, added to the challenges and the ripples of disturbance continue. Manufacturers struggled, sponsorship constricted, teams shed riders and some have even had to pull out of some competition altogether.

Tough times never last forever though and just like a rider coming back from injury, the industry will dig deep and focus on looking forward. It'll make improvements, build momentum, get back to full fitness and go beyond. It'll be better, fitter and stronger than before.

The positive foundations and fundamentals of the sport are undeniable. It is steeped in agreeable attributes. It is relatable and identifiable. There's culture, community and camaraderie.

It's even a mesmerising spectacle to those who don't ride. Clare Balding's comments about being riveted while watching the DH World Champs speak volumes about the potential wider appeal of the sport.

I hope every element of the sport and the industry can pull together and share the spoils so that the whole thing can flourish for everyone who loves it.

As I'm writing this final chapter, winter is releasing its grip here in the Portes du Soleil. As it does and as the snow disappears, our minds are shifting to bikes and a long season of riding beckon provocatively ahead. "*Yay!*"

Writing this book has kicked off so many more plans and ideas of mountain bike-related things I'd like to do, places I want to go and trails I'm keen to ride.

T-Dog has signed up for his first official season of sanctioned DH racing in France so we'll be away for a few fun race weekenders. They've just announced that the UCI World Cup DH and XC are returning to Les Gets in 2024 and that the Enduro will be held again in the Portes du Soleil. Can't wait for all that and I'll definitely be checking out more of the enduro this year!

Baz and the lads are looking at dates for a trip over and my mates who were out of action last year are all well on the road to recovery. It'd be really nice to catch up with my bro, have a trip down memory lane and return to ride some old favourites as well.

Ooo! And we've just pencilled in a trip to Finale in two weeks to kick it all off. *"Wahoo!"*

Mountain biking has been a major factor shaping the course of my life. It's been the catalyst and vehicle for many good times with many sound people. It has brought me so many positive benefits in so many ways. Whilst I stay pretty fit all year round, I never feel fitter, stronger, leaner and harder than at the end of the bike season. I love it!

We all share the same experiences. The same trails, the same sensations and we're lucky to spend our time outside and connected to nature.

I've done quite a bit of thanking here and there throughout this book and seriously, cheers to all you guys and fellow riders, for all your contributions to the sport and for sharing the love.

Mountain biking is a sport with a deep soul that exposes us to so many things that are good in life, and when something is good, it's worth taking a moment to truly appreciate it.

It's great to celebrate things that connect and unite people in the world, things that focus our energy in positive directions. On top of everything else, mountain biking does just that, and what's even better is that it does it by delivering sheer joy through pure fun.

SEND IT!

33 - An Ode to Mountain Biking

There's a tug within that's hard to resist.
A whisper in mind that insists to persist.

It's the pull, the draw and the call to arms,
To straddle your rig and succumb to its charms.

It takes perseverance and patience to build your skill,
then commitment and courage to step up and fulfil.

Risk, reward, resilience and resolve.
Challenges, progression and technique to evolve.

Concentration and focus merge to Zen-like flow,
and there's a voice of intuition, that it's useful to know.

We need fitness, strength and explosive power,
tempered with precision and finesse for hour after hour.

There's speed, aggression, a dangerous air,
balanced with artistry, style and personal flair.

Gems of engineering lead us away,
to the mountains and woods for good times and play.

There's the trails, the travel, the thrills and the spills,

FOR THE LOVE OF MOUNTAIN BIKING

the connection to nature as we rip through the hills.

There's a bond amongst and a connection inside.
A vibe in the tribe that's hard to describe.

Concerns and worries melt away,
replaced with excitement and glee 'til the end of the day.

Is there any better pursuit for us to employ,
for freedom and fun and pure inner joy.

Glossary

Some of the words or phrases in this book may not make much sense, or even officially exist. If there's any confusion, the following glossary should hopefully clear it up:

Ace - Something particularly good; awesome; excellent; brilliant.

Aggy - Aggressive.

Amplitude - The size of an air or jump.

Awesome - Excellent; brilliant; fantastic.

Backed - Backflip.

Backflip - Backflip.

Bap - Nope, not a bread bun from Yorkshire. A descriptive noise and sensation of riding over roots.

Bar-spin - Completely spinning the handlebars and front wheel around one or more times whilst airing a jump. Requires single crown forks and modifications to cabling.

Berm - A bank built on the outside of a corner to increase cornering speed, flow and fun.

Biggy - A big one; no biggy as in no big deal.

Bikeporn - Images and videos of bikes, equipment and action that elicit a heightened state of positive emotion and desire.

Blat - A quick fast ride.

Blast - A ride.

Blowing out of your backside - Breathing very hard.

Bum Sticks - Fiddlesticks; crumbs; dammit.

Bunny Hop - Using the bike's suspension and body movement to jump the bike and rider into the air.

Can Can - Taking one foot off the pedal whilst airing a jump and kicking it over the top tube to the other side of the bike before returning to land.

Clocked - Spotted; saw/seen.

Coaster Wheelie - Balancing on the back wheel, whilst descending, seated, without pedalling, and using the back brake to maintain the balance point.

Come-a-cropper - Fail; fall off.

Cruumph - Noise.

Divvy - Nitwit; moron; plonker; numpty.

Double Jump - A jump with a dip (but not a gap) between the take off and landing.

Don Mega - Best of the best.

Endo - Like a wheelie but lifting the rear wheel and riding on the front one.

Features - Usually man-made additions to a trail that add challenge and interest: jumps; bridges; gantries; step-ups; step-downs; rock gardens etc.

Fessed-up - Confessed.

Filter Feature - A feature that is designed to act as a gauge of what others are ahead on a trail.

Floaty - A jump or air which gives a sensation of extended airtime.

Flowy - A smooth, fast-running trail, state of mind or physical state.

Flow - A smooth, fast-running trail, state of mind or physical state.

FOMO - Fear of missing out.

Four-Cross - 4X; 4 Cross; A race format where four participants compete on a track wide enough to accommodate them. Can also refer to the track itself.

Freakin'(g) - Flipping; blinking; particularly; especially.

Freeride - Read chapter 19 big-boy/girl/person, read the chapter.

Frothing - Extremely excited.

Full Tilt - As fast as possible.

Full Lick - As fast as possible.

Full Chat - As fast as possible.

Full Pelt - As fast as possible.

Full Send - As fast, high or far as possible.

Full Charge - As fast as possible.

Full Bore - As fast as possible.

Full "…" - It's probably safe that anything starting with "full" means "as fast as possible".

Gap Jump - Jump where there is a gap between take-off and landing. Coming up short will most likely be unpleasant.

Get - Old English word meaning annoying person; berk; sod. Considered a milder term than "git".

Git - Old English word meaning unpleasant or annoying person. Harsher than "get".

Gnar - Hardcore; extreme; challenging; awesome.

Gnarly - Hardcore; extreme; challenging; awesome.

Hero Dirt - Slightly damp, packed, fast, grippy, trail dirt that instils confidence and can make you ride like an absolute hero.

Hip - A jump where the landing is at a different angle and direction to the take off requiring rotation and alignment in the air. Usually 90 degrees.

Hooned - Riding with maximum speed, stoke and a degree of abandon.

Huck - Making an effort to send an extra big jump.

Lasses - Girls or young women.

Lifty (Lifties, multiple) - A mechanical lift operator or supervisor. Controls the function and customer use of cable cars, chairlifts, etc.

Line(s) - The route your wheels take.

Manifestal - Totally made up by J3 Sedbergh primary school students many moons ago. Means Awesome. Didn't catch on with the rest of the world. Unless it was shortened to Manifest(ing). "Hmmmmm?"

Manual - Balancing and riding on the back wheel without pedalling.

Mega - Awesome.

Moniker - Name.

MTB - Mountain bike/mountain biking.

North Shore - Raised wooden bridges and tracks.

Nac Nac - Taking one foot off the pedal whilst airing a jump and kicking it over the rear wheel to the other side of the bike before returning to land.

No-Hander Lander - Landing a jump without returning hands to the bars.

Nuff - Enough

One Footer - Taking one foot off the pedal whilst airing a jump.

Phew - An expression of relief.

Pingy - An extra springy sensation.

Ping - An extra springy sensation.

Pre Hop - Bunny hopping before a down slope to jump quickly and smoothly over the lip and into the transition.

Pull - Making extra effort to launch the bike into the air on take off. May be required for a big jump or the result a last-minute recalculation of jump size and current speed.

Pump - Weighting and unweighting the bike over dips, rises and corners in the trail to build speed and momentum without pedalling.

Rail - Riding a berm corner or trail at high speed as if you were on a rail.

Reet - Alight, as in "It'll be alright"… "It'll be reet."

Roller - A hump in the trail. Size may vary.

Sanga - Sandwich.

Sarnie - Sandwich.

Send - Going for a jump with full commitment.

Send It - Just do it! Go for it! Commit! Whether it's a jump, drop, trail or gap. Go for it with full commitment.

Scoof - A sound that sounds like scoof.

Schiz-ed - Short for a minor fleeting schizophrenic type episode. Hopefully not a cancellable term now.

Schralp - Turning sharply in a corner so that the rear wheel breaks traction sideways without braking. Not a skid.

Shapers - People who build and maintain the trails.

Shaping Crew - The team of people who build and maintain the trails.

Shizzle - Euphemism for "shit" and especially "the shit." Wide use attributed to Snoop D, O, double G.

Sod It/Sod That - Expression of annoyance; never mind! Forget about it!

Spondoolies - Money

Squirrel Catcher - Filter feature designed as a gauge of the trail difficulty ahead.

Steeze - A combination of style and ease. Super-chilled style.

Step Down - A jump where the landing is lower than the take off.

Step Up - A jump where the landing is higher than the take off.

Suicide No-Hander - Taking hands completely off the bars whilst airing a jump and extending arms backwards behind the body before returning them to the bars to land.

Sweet - Awesome

Switchback - Sharp hairpin style bend that almost doubles back on itself.

Table Top - A jump with a flat, level top between the take off and landing.

Tart Up - Improve the appearance of.

Trucking On - Travelling at considerable speed.

T-Bog - Trick whilst airing a jump. Taking one hand off the bars and grabbing the front of the seat whilst twisting the bars with the other. Returning everything to the start position to land.

Wee Snifter - A Scottish term for a small glass of whisky.

Wahoo - An expression of elation.

Wheelie - Balancing on the back wheel whilst pedalling.

Whip - Turning the bike sideways whilst airing a jump so that the rear wheel whips out to the side.

Whooomph - A Noise.

Wickle - Little

Yeat - Putting extra effort into a jump.

FOR THE LOVE OF MOUNTAIN BIKING

Find all the latest news and links to social media channels on James's website:

WWW.JAMESIE.LIFE

Made in the USA
Monee, IL
03 October 2024

6ac2140b-8314-4825-a7a1-5a44198e747cR02